CAN DOESN'T MEAN SHOULD

Essential Knowledge for 21st Century Parents

Paul Smolen, MD

Edited by Wendy and Benjamin Smolen

Torchflame Books
An imprint of Light Messages

Published 2015, by Torchflame Books
   an Imprint of Light Messages
www.lightmessages.com
Durham, NC 27713 USA
SAN: 920-9298

Paperback ISBN: 978-1-61153-138-1
Ebook ISBN: 978-1-61153-136-7

CONTENTS

INTRODUCTION

Today's parents face decisions that no parents have previously had to face. The dizzying pace of change and innovation in the 21st century makes raising children a scary endeavor. Our great grandparents grappled with decisions unaffected by the intrusion of modern life and technology into the family. Today's parents must cope with the realities of modern life. These include the scary world of the Internet; the lure of smartphones and tablets; the seductive and violent media messages that our culture promotes; the availability of highly processed but minimally nutritious foods; the new phenomenon of children having access to large amounts of money; and hyper-competitive academic and extracurricular environments. How do parents learn enough about these subjects to make the right decisions for their children and family?

My Goal:

Most parents today can provide much of what modern life has to offer, but the real question is *should* they? That question is the crux of this book. In the subsequent chapters, my goal is to give parents knowledge and insight into the issues presented to empower them to determine what is best for their families. My goal is to help parents navigate the minefield of the can/should decisions they face. Knowledge and the confidence to make the best decisions for our families are the keys to unlocking the great parent in all of us.

My Qualifications:

I have practiced pediatrics for 36 years; I have spent my entire adult life with young children and families. I log about 5000 office visits a year, so over the course of my career I have had more than 160,000 patient encounters…and those were just during daylight hours! My experience as a "seasoned" pediatrician has given me a unique vantage from which to observe parents struggle with the can/should dilemmas inherent in life today.

My job involves recognizing serious disease when it presents itself, but also listening, observing, advising, counseling, directing, cheerleading, and encouraging. I have had the opportunity to be part of thousands of conversations about the subjects addressed in this book, including: what is the optimal nutrition for children; does screen time have an influence on children; what is the role of chores and household responsibilities in shaping the character of children; and how do parents find the right balance between academics, extra-curricular activities, and free unstructured play? Each of these scenarios entails can/should decisions. I can do or provide this or that, but should I, and if so, how much and under what circumstances?

I have paid close attention to the myriad of parents and families with whom I have had the privilege to be associated. I have an extremely intimate, front row seat to the workings of families with their attendant strengths, weakness, challenges, and difficulties. Over the long course of my practice, I have gained a tremendous respect for parents. In my opinion, it takes character, physical strength, a loving heart, and determination to be a successful parent. Consider just a few of the tasks that parents must master:

- Feeding and protecting their children.
- Providing shelter for their little ones.
- Shaping their children's character.

- Setting limits for children's behavior both inside and outside the home.
- Teaching children right from wrong.
- Demanding honesty and accountability in their children.
- Fostering a sense of community and service to others.
- Creating opportunities for their children to thrive.
- Getting their children educated and capable of a self-sustaining life.
- Helping their children find their own life's interest and talents.
- Setting a good example for children to follow.

As the sun begins to set on my career, it is time to articulate my perspective on many issues that parents will face. Much of this book will consist of my opinions, but they are based on observation and experience. I include science and facts whenever possible to help you in your own thought process— to help you with your own can/should decisions.

Paul Smolen, MD

ACKNOWLEDGMENTS

I would like to thank those that inspired and helped me create this book: my wife Wendy and my son Benjamin, both of whom provided advice, superb editing skills guidance, support, and patience throughout the book's creation; my nephew Seth Jaffe, the rocketman barrister who helped me with technical advice; Stephen Valder M.D., John Plonk M.D., Anne Gessner PNP, Ashley Grimm RN, Annie Beth Donahue, Charlotte Rouchouze, Dean Brodhag, Stephanie and Sophie Gardner, Megan Schlie, Ellis Chase, Michele Orwin, and David Ross-- all of who graciously contributed effort to the creation of this book.

Paul Smolen, MD

CHAPTER ONE
Parenting Then and Now

The New Reality of Parenting:
Change at the Speed of Light.

The pace of change in today's world is mind-boggling; our great grandparents would barely recognize life today. Even our language would baffle our grandmothers. Can you imagine saying, "Hey, grandma, I'm *running* down to the *Quick Pick* to *grab* some *munchies* and an *energy drink*. Be back in a *flash*." Oh, what a hundred years can do to language, culture and lifestyle. Never before in human history has change occurred at such a rapid pace.

In many respects, children at the turn of the century had a drastically different childhood experience than those born today. Children born in 1900 were likely to be raised in a rural setting, surrounded by farms, mostly in single-family households and raised by two parents.[1] A child's days were often long and hard. Children were an important source of labor for their families and communities. As part of their families, their living expenses were already paid, they were strong, and they had good stamina. Today's school calendar is a reflection of just how important their labor was to a family and community. Children worked both at home, on

---

[1]Caplow, Theodore, Louis Hicks, and Ben J. Wattenberg. The First Measured Century. (Washington: AEI Press, 2001), 12-13.

farms, and in the growing industrialized world. With their days divided up among household chores, schoolwork, and work in their communities, children in 1900 had little free time. Summers did not provide vacation or free time; rather they provided time to work.

Education beyond basic high school was rare.[2] Most families owned few books, the Bible being the most influential one. In 1900, there were 6000 new books published. By 1997, that number had increased 1000 fold to 65,000.[3] While some children in 1900 learned to read, 10.7% of children were functionally illiterate.[4] Family and church were the major influences as their minds developed. Most families had limited access to world news or opinion. Of course, conventional radio and TV did not yet exit. Many children may not have ever had the opportunity to travel more than 25 miles from home their entire lives. Photography was in its infancy and out of reach for most families. Pictures of people and events were rare and precious in 1900.

Participation in organized sports and extracurricular activities was a luxury. Only the children of the very affluent had an opportunity to learn to play tennis or golf, or even how to swim. Consequently, death by drowning was a common event among the children of 1900. The average child had little access to cultural events such as orchestral music or live theater. Even reading a newspaper or a magazine was an oddity for most children. Those adults in the community with the most formal education provided academic training. High school graduation rates hovered around thirteen percent. College graduation rates were extremely low as well, about three percent.[5]

---

[2]Ibid.

[3]Ibid, 266-267.

[4]The National Center for Education Statistics. "Rate of Illiteracy circa 1900." <http://nces.ed.gov/naal/lit_history.asp>.

[5]*Caplow,* 53-53.

Most families were much larger in 1900: the average family consisted of six people.[6] Living space was limited, and free time was the exception, not the rule. Household income was only a fraction of what today's average families enjoy. In 1999 dollars, the average income of the bottom 40 percent of Americans has tripled since 1929, while the income of the top five percent of Americans income has doubled. On average, families in 1998 had three times more money to spend compared to families in 1929.[7]

Transportation in 1900 was by foot, bike, wagon, and horse. There were no internal combustion engines, no cars, and no motorized tractors. Human and animal power were the engines of the time. Electricity--and all of the devices it now runs--was simply not available.[8] Only the rich enjoyed indoor plumbing.

Packaged, processed foods did not exist in 1900. Everything was fresh. Most food was locally grown and consumed. Because only limited refrigeration was possible, food that was produced had to be consumed immediately. The only foods that could be stored or transported long distances were dry foods like grains, dried fruits, nuts, and salted or cured meats. Poverty was abundant and food was often scarce. Access to seasonal fruits and vegetables in areas where they were not grown was extremely limited. In other words, in 1900, food didn't come from a factory; rather, it was produced on a farm and consumed locally.

Fast-forward 100 years to the 21st century: 100 years made an enormous difference. Over the course of the 20th Century, life for children improved exponentially. Greater wealth for the average family accompanied urban living and the industrialization of manufacturing. Increased family wealth unlocked a myriad of opportunities for children, the

---

[6]Ibid, 84-85.
[7]Ibid, 164-165.
[8]Ibid, 98-99.

most important of which was the opportunity to go to school. Education began to be seen as a right and a necessity, not a luxury. The right to go to school for a basic education and was eventually codified into law. In 1852, Massachusetts became the first state to require education for children beginning at age six. Not until 1918 did the last state, Mississippi, institute mandatory education.[9] Along with mandatory education, states banned or limited child labor.

Throughout the 20th century, as the wealth of families gradually grew, children certainly benefited, enjoying less physical work, more devices of convenience, more spending money, and more venues for entertainment than ever before. Additionally, 20th century America witnessed a dramatic decrease in infant mortality, a remarkable increase in the average life span, the disappearance of most of the dreaded childhood illnesses, access to an abundance of food, access to educational opportunities for most, access to health care, improved quality of housing (including reliable heating and cooling), communication and travel across long distances, and an abundant amount of free time.[10]

Many unintended consequences accompanied these incredible improvements in lifestyle.

Unfortunately, in addition to wonderful improvements in life style, the 20th century also ushered in some unexpected, unfortunate consequences, many of which we are just beginning to understand. The Cans of the 20th century are beginning to catch up with our children. Undeniably, children became much healthier during the past 100 years, but a new set of health problems has replaced previous diseases. Most doctors in the Western World have probably never seen a case of polio, diphtheria, or tetanus, but daily they see cases

---

[9]Info Please. "State Compulsory School Attendance Laws." <http://www.infoplease.com/ipa/A0112617.html>.

[10]*Caplow, 134-135*

of adult-onset diabetes, depression and anxiety, obesity, sleep problems, asthma, and hypertension...in children! How could this be? What is going on? We find the answers in our indulgence in the cans of the 20th century. We can drive our children most places rather than require them to walk. We can fill their free time with academics and screen time rather than unstructured active play. We can allow our children to eat a diet rich in sugar, fat, and salt instead of the healthier diet that our forbearers ate. Finally, families often can afford to give their children disposable money to spend rather than encouraging them to earn their spending money and to practice thrift.

Parents create the reality that their children experience.

We have seen how the past 100 years have unleashed a lifestyle that few could have imagined in 1900. Everywhere we turn today, we have a new can offered to our children. Today it may be portable screens, but who knows what will be next? The question for our generation is where to draw the line between can and should. You as parents create the world that your children live in, and this book is a guide to creating a world that has a balance between can and should. All of the Cans available to our children have potentially serious, unintended consequences.

Some of my readers may conclude that I want families to live the life of colonial times. Nothing could be further from the truth. In most respects, the 20th century improved almost everyone's lives. I hope that we continue to innovate, discover, educate, and cure. We do, however, need to recalibrate modern life. I hope that after reading this book you will feel more confident and informed when making decisions for your children. I want you to dive into the world of parenting with your eyes wide open, informed, and thinking clearly.

The discussions that are going to unfold in each of the next eight chapters are my attempt to present you with up-to-date information about a range of topics you need to deal

11

with. I call these topics 'spheres.' Each sphere is an aspect of family life where you need to make can/should decisions. You have a lot of power to shape your child's early experience. It's in everyone's interest for that childhood experience to be as healthy and positive as possible. Here is a quick summary of the questions we will address in this book:

- Parents can serve children ultra-processed foods. Should they?

- Parents can entertain and divert children with screens. Should they?

- Parents can give children access to large amounts of disposable money. Should they?

- Parents can exempt children from daily household work and responsibility. Should they?

- Parents can spend large amounts of money, energy, and time providing intensified academic and extracurricular activities for your children. Should you?

✓ The childhood experience has changed drastically in the past 100 years.

✓ Growing wealth, technology, competition for success, and leisure time have created, at times, an unhealthy environment for children.

✓ Balancing many of the cans available to children with what they should experience is the modern parent's dilemma.

CHAPTER TWO
Sphere #1: Nutrition

**Your child's choices in food should be between
good and great—no junk served in this kitchen!**

One of the most important tasks parents have is to feed their young. Sustenance is right up there with shelter and protection from danger, yet few parents are nutritionists. Many parents know little about nutrition and almost nothing about how their child's diet may affect his or her health. This fact is borne out by the fact that if children today bore labels based on what they eat, their top five ingredients would be grain-based desserts (such as cake), pizza, apple juice and other sweetened beverages, chicken pieces such as nuggets, and bread.[11] The USDA chart below describes what most American children eat.[12] They eat a shocking amount of low quality food. Of the top 25 foods consumed by children ages two to eighteen years, the only vegetables listed are white potatoes; the only fruits listed are fruit drink and fruit juice. Fruits and vegetables should be the mainstay of a child's diet, yet American children rarely consume them.

---

[11]Fox, Mary Kay, M.Ed; Susan Pac, M.S., R.D.; Barbara Devaney, PhD; Linda Jankowski, M.S. "Feeding Infants and Toddlers Study: What Foods Are Infants and Toddlers Eating?" Journal of the American Dietician Association (2004).

[12]United States. USDA: Dietary Guidelines for Americans 2010. Washington: GPO, 2010. Table 1, page 12.

Top Ten Foods Consumed by Children in the US
- Grain based desserts (138 Kcal/day)
- Pizza (136 Kcal/day)
- Soda/Energy/Sports drinks (118 Kcal/day)
- Yeast Breads (114 kcal/day)
- Chicken and Chicken mixed dishes (113 Kcal/day)
- Pasta and pasta dishes (91 Kcal/day)
- Reduced fat milk (86 Kcal/day)
- Dairy desserts (76 Kcal/day)
- Potato/corn/chips (70 Kcal/day)
- Ready to eat cereals (65 Kcal/day)

How can a child's body grow and mature with such nutrient-poor food for fuel? Babies and children need nutrient-rich food to enable reliable cell division, growth, and function. Food not only maintains their bodies--it powers their growth. Unless those cells have all the macro and micronutrients they need, things go wrong. We pediatricians see what happens when mothers or babies are deficient in folic acid, for example: birth defects such as spina bifida, a major birth defect of the brain and spine. Babies deficient in iron can suffer cognitive impairment and a higher risk of pneumonia and other serious infections.[13] Vitamin D deficiency may result in a crippling bone disorder called 'rickets' as well as an increased risk of diabetes, autoimmune diseases, and multiple sclerosis.[14] The allergy epidemic we are currently seeing in the United

---

[13]Fox, Mary Kay, M.Ed; Susan Pac, M.S., R.D.; Barbara Devaney, PhD; Linda Jankowski, M.S. "Feeding Infants and Toddlers Study: What Foods Are Infants and Toddlers Eating?" Journal of the American Dietician Association (2004).

[14]Fox, Mary Kay, M.Ed; Susan Pac, M.S., R.D.; Barbara Devaney, PhD; Linda Jankowski, M.S. "Feeding Infants and Toddlers Study: What Foods Are Infants and Toddlers Eating?" Journal of the American Dietician Association (2004).

States may be food generated as well.[15] [16] Food is extremely important to a child's well being. Providing a healthy diet for children is fundamental to good parenting. Parents cannot cut corners when it comes to providing wholesome, whole foods for their children.

Industrialization of food in the twentieth century.

The twentieth century provided plenty of food for most of the population; unfortunately, this progress came at the cost of diminished food quality. The industrialization of food production lowered its quality and changed the natural balance of nutrients in food. As food became cheaper, more available, with longer and longer shelf life, more processing was introduced into food production. Efficiency and low cost is what the American consumer demanded, and efficiency and low cost is what the food industry delivered. Unfortunately, many of the practices that we have come to accept as part of food production are now proving to be less than ideal: rapid growth of crops in nutrient-poor soil; industrialization of animal husbandry; the use of pesticides and plastic packaging; and the addition of artificial colors, flavors, sugars, and salt, to mention a few. These new food production methods have profoundly changed our diets, sometimes in harmful ways.

> Efficiency and low cost is what the
> American consumer demanded, and
> efficiency and low cost is what the food
> industry delivered.

[15]Fox, Mary Kay, M.Ed; Susan Pac, M.S., R.D.; Barbara Devaney, PhD; Linda Jankowski, M.S. "Feeding Infants and Toddlers Study: What Foods Are Infants and Toddlers Eating?" Journal of the American Dietician Association (2004).

[16]Fox, Mary Kay, M.Ed; Susan Pac, M.S., R.D.; Barbara Devaney, PhD; Linda Jankowski, M.S. "Feeding Infants and Toddlers Study: What Foods Are Infants and Toddlers Eating?" Journal of the American Dietician Association (2004).

Good food builds strong children.

Medical literature demonstrates the realization that food quality has an important impact on our long-term health. Our grandmothers sent their children outdoors for some sunshine and fresh air, made sure they got enough sleep, and provided a balanced variety of food. Medical researchers affirm our grandmothers' wisdom: Vitamin D deficiency (prevented by sunshine and fresh air) is at the core of so many diseases and cures; sleep deprivation has terribly destructive effects on our brains and vascular system; and foods that contain high fructose corn syrup, excess salt, and artificial preservatives and colors have serious, degenerative effects. Cutting edge medical research is finding out what everyone a hundred years ago knew: "Good food builds strong children."

How is processed food different than real or whole food?

What do experts mean by the term "processed food"? How does it differ from "whole food"? The answers are not always self-evident. For example, we can argue that cavemen processed food by drying meats and sweetening foods with honey. Even the simple process of cooking food with heat is arguably a form of processing. Intuitively, we all understand that this type of minimal processing doesn't harm the quality of the food in a significant way. Let us consider today's modern food processing methods. Without these modern food preparation procedures, we probably could not feed our population. Some degree of processing is essential to maintaining our population. As our thinking evolves about processed foods, the concept of "lightly processed" versus "ultra-processed" is beginning to take hold. Lightly processed foods are foods created using essentially intact ingredients with high nutritional value; these foods are combined in ways that don't drastically alter their natural ingredients or change their nutritional value. Ultra-processed foods are exactly the opposite: their ingredients are markedly different from the original sources from which they were grown, and they are combined in a way that drastically alters the balance and availability of nutrients. Compare a can of high quality potato soup versus a bag of potato chips. The potato soup has been processed from the original potato: it has been peeled, boiled at 212°F, seasoned, mixed with milk, and canned to keep it from spoiling. The potato chip, on the other hand, has been peeled, sliced, deep fried in extremely hot oil (350°F or higher), dried, salted, and combined with preservatives, artificial colors, and artificial flavors. The potato chip, unlike the potato soup, is an ultra-processed food. Both foods began with potatoes, but the nutrition of the end product varies drastically as a result of the amount of "processing" that occurs. Most of us would agree that potato soup is a nutritious product, whereas we categorize potato chips as junk food due to the addition of large amounts of salt and fat, artificial flavors, and preservatives.

What does the evidence show about deleterious effects of processed food?

Since this book concerns infants and children, we should start with a comparison of infant formula versus breast milk. Here we have an opportunity to see how a highly processed food (infant formula) stacks up against a totally natural, unprocessed food (breast milk). To be fair, evidence shows that breastfed infants experience, on average, more intense newborn jaundice, a major health concern for newborns in the first weeks of life, and are at greater risk of vitamin D deficiency during infancy.[17] [18] [19] These problems may have

---

[17]Holick, Michael F., M.D., Ph.D. "Vitamin D Deficiency." New England Journal of Medicine 357 (July 2007): 266-281 <http://www.nejm.org/doi/full/10.1056/NEJMra070553>.

[18]Bertini, Giovanna, Carlo Dani, Michele Tronchin, Firmino F. Rubaltelli. "Is Breastfeeding Really Favoring Early Neonatal Jaundice?" Pediatrics 107 (March 2001): 41. <http://www.pediatricsdigest.mobi/content/107/3/e41.short>.

[19]United States. Centers for Disease Control. Vitamin D Supplementation and Breasting. Washington: GPO, 2009. <http://www.cdc.gov/breastfeeding/recommendations/vitamin_d.html>.

more to do with our modern indoor lifestyle than with an inherent deficiency in breast milk. Aside from these problems, however, breastfeeding leads in every category: less chance an infant will develop food allergy, healthier immune function, less obesity, stronger bonding with mom, better bone mineralization, better vision, and better cognitive function on average.[20] Note that some of these health parameters, such as food allergy and obesity, are short-term measures whereas some, such as cognitive functioning, are long term. Breast milk seems to outpace infant formula in both the short and long term health outcomes. What's not to love about breast milk? Even the formula companies admit that breast milk is the preferred food for a human baby. Formula is an adequate substitute when mom's milk is unavailable, but it is not an equal replacement.

Do diet excesses cause disease?

For centuries, astute observers have suspected that the types and quality of the food we consume or fail to consume have an impact on our health. First, we discovered that certain nutritional deficiencies cause diseases like scurvy (an illness caused by a lack of vitamin C) and pellagra (a disease caused by a lack of the B vitamin niacin). In the 20th century, researchers studying a population in Framingham, Massachusetts discovered that coronary heart disease seemed to be linked to an elevated cholesterol level in the blood and that this disease process begins in infancy and young adult life, finally manifesting its deleterious effects in the third decade of life and beyond.[21] This observation ignited the search for dietary factors that eventually lead to degenerative diseases

---

[20]American Academy of Pediatrics. "Policy Statement: Breastfeeding and the Use of Human Milk." Pediatrics 115 (2012): 496.

[21]Fox, Mary Kay, M.Ed; Susan Pac, M.S., R.D.; Barbara Devaney, PhD; Linda Jankowski, M.S. "Feeding Infants and Toddlers Study: What Foods Are Infants and Toddlers Eating?" Journal of the American Dietician Association (2004).

(diseases of aging) such as vascular disease, liver diseases like cirrhosis, or even colon and breast cancers.

Today, most physicians accept the tenet that certain diets accelerate degenerative diseases such as cancer and coronary heart disease.[22] They also accept the opposite belief: that certain diets can retard the aging process and the development of degenerative diseases. Examples of these diets include the "Mediterranean diet" and the "DASH diet."[23] [24]

How should parents use this information about the effect of diet on disease? What do parents need to know about nutrition to avoid health problems in their children? Three major concepts come into play in answering that question:

- Diets that have an excess of any nutrient over a long time are likely to accelerate or cause disease.

- Diets deficient in nutrients over a long period of time are likely to accelerate or cause disease.

- Diets high in artificial and highly processed ingredients, consumed over a long period of time, are likely to accelerate or cause disease.

Diets that have an excess of any nutrient over a long time are likely to accelerate or cause disease.

Diabetes is the prototypic disease in this category. Excess sugar intake eventually may overload a child's ability to metabolize sugar, and type 2 diabetes (also known as insulin

---

[22]Trichopoulou, Antonia, M.D., Tina Costacou, Ph.D., Christina Bamia, Ph.D., and Dimitrios Trichopoulos, M.D. "Adherence to a Mediterranean Diet and Survival in a Greek Population." New England Journal Medicine 348 (June 26, 2003): 348:2599-2608. <http://www.nejm.org/doi/full/10.1056/NEJMoa025039>.

[23]Fung et al. "Incidence of and Mortality From Coronary Heart Disease and Stroke in Women." Circulation 119 (2009): 1093-1100.

[24]Singh, et al. "Effect of Indo-Mediterranean Diet on Progression of Coronary Artery Disease in High Risk Patients." 360 (November 2002): 1455-1461.

resistant diabetes) eventually sets in. A person with Type 2 diabetes has cells that literally stop responding to the hormonal message that insulin delivers: i.e., "Cell, take up glucose from the blood and store it in fat cells or burn it." Certainly there are genetics at play when someone develops type 2 diabetes, but the biggest factor in determining whether a child or an adult develops diabetes is whether he or she indulges in a persistent, long-term intake of high amounts of sugar. Sugar includes glucose, fructose, lactose, and any other sugar. Sugar comes in the form of soda, sweet cereals, and breakfast foods designed for children, as well as desserts, candy, and sugar added into processed foods.[25] [26] The average American child aged four to eight years consumes about 22 teaspoons of sugar a day, far above the recommended daily allowance of four to eight teaspoons.[27] This table from a recent article tracking added sugar intake of Americans demonstrates the problem we face:[28]

Sugar intake of American children by age expressed in kilocalories[29]

Average Kcal Sugar Intake Boys/Girls	Sugar Intake 2-5 year olds Boys/Girls	Sugar Intake 6-11 year olds Boys/Girls	Sugar Intake 12-19 year olds Boys/Girls
362/282	218/196	345/293	442/314

Recommended daily intake of added sugar is 64-128 kilocalories

---

[25]Johnson, et al. "Dietary Sugars Intake and Cardiovascular Health." Circulation 20:11 (September 15, 2009): 1011-1020.

[26]Smolen, Paul, M.D. "Why Your Child Should Avoid Sugary Drinks." DocSmo.com <http://www.docsmo.com/why-your-child-should-avoid-sugary-drinks>.

[27]United States. Centers for Disease Control. Consumption of Added Sugar Among U.S. Children and Adolescents. Washington: GPO, 2012.

[28]Ibid.

[29]CDC/NCHS, National Health and Nutrition Examination Survey, 2005-2008

Physicians and public health officials are beginning to understand the consequences of an excess intake of sugar throughout childhood: adult diseases that were unheard of in children are becoming commonplace. In addition to insulin-resistant type 2 diabetes (formerly known as 'adult onset'), these include elevated cholesterol levels, hypertension, obesity, skeletal stress injuries, and non-infectious hepatitis or NASH (nonalcoholic steatohepatitis).[30] Too much salt, sugar, fat, and calories seem to be the bases of all of these diseases.

Diets deficient in nutrients over a long period are likely to accelerate or cause disease.

Ironically, many children are deficient in a variety of nutrients, despite easy access to plenty of food. Nutritional deficiencies are particularly common among American teenagers. Iron deficiency, inadequate calcium and fiber intake, as well as vitamin D deficiency are almost epidemic today among American teens. This fact is not surprising considering that a full 33% of the food an American child consumes today is served away from home.[31] [32] Most American children eat breakfast and/or lunch at school and supper at fast food or other restaurants. A shocking 41% of America's teens eat fast food daily![33] Unfortunately, many of these meals, while satisfying, are deficient in many micronutrients. We are just beginning to learn about the plethora of diseases that can be linked to chronic nutritional deficiencies. Here is a partial list of the more common deficiencies and their health consequences:

---

[30]Ibid.
[31]Ibid.
[32]Ibid.
[33]Ibid.

Vitamin D and calcium deficiency and insufficiency

- Definite Links: Rickets, weakened bones and metabolic problems with calcium metabolism, muscle weakness.

- Suspected Links: Adult onset diabetes, allergies, multiple sclerosis, cancers of various sorts.

Iron deficiency

- Definite Link: Cognitive impairment in children, higher risk of pneumonia and other infections, and sleep problems.

Fiber deficiency

- Definite Link: Constipation, obesity, fluctuations in blood sugar.

- Suspected Link: Diverticulitis in adult life, colon cancer, elevated blood fats including cholesterol, coronary heart disease.

Diets with lots of artificial and highly processed ingredients, consumed over a long period of time, are likely to accelerate or cause disease.

A growing body of evidence demonstrates that inflammatory illnesses such as food allergies, inhalant allergy, eczema, and asthma may be linked to diet.[34] Researchers believe that certain foods, processed in particular ways, may switch on a child's immune system with a response known as 'allergic inflammation.' Common examples of allergic inflammation are (infant formula) milk and soy colitis in babies, anaphylactic response to peanut and other foods, allergic esophagitis (an historically unheard of diagnosis), and celiac disease (a once rare but now common allergic inflammation to a protein found in many grains called 'gluten'). Does the

---

[34]Mccann, D. "Food Additives and Hyperactive Behaviour in 3 year olds and 8/9 year old children in the Community; randomized, double-blinded, placebo trial." Lancet 117 (2008) 1216-1217.

food we eat differ from that our grandparents ate, or are we different, irritated by strange proteins, fats, preservatives, and chemicals used in foods today? Scientists have no definite answers to these questions. What we do know for sure, however, is that these inflammatory diseases are happening more often than in the past, and the cause likely has something to do with modern agricultural and food processing techniques.

Equally alarming is a growing body of evidence linking food preservatives and colors to cognitive problems in children. Certain children with ADHD, for example, become less impulsive and improve in their ability to concentrate, pay attention, and follow directions when food preservatives and dyes are removed from their diets.[35]

The 21st century confronts parents with a slew of can/should decisions with respect to feeding children. Our grandmothers would not recognize as food most of the processed foods that are readily available to our children. We owe it to ourselves and our children to learn about these foods and their impact on our health. I suggest the following goals for you to consider:

- Breastfeed infants for as long as possible.
- Buy the highest quality food you can afford.
- Most of a child's food should consist of fruits and vegetables.
- Minimize ultra-processed foods.
- Minimize sugar intake (including at the table).
- Minimize chemicals in your food (fresh foods are best).
- Create variety in everyone's diet.
- Children should eat what you eat.
- Set a good example for your children by eating a good diet yourself.

---

[35]Mccann, D. "Food Additives and Hyperactive Behaviour in 3 year olds and 8/9 year old children in the Community; randomized, double-blinded, placebo trial." Lancet 117 (2008) 1216-1217.

- Eat together and at home whenever possible.
- Don't forbid unhealthy foods, just allow limited access to them.

Can/should nutrition decisions that you must confront:

- You can feed your babies infant formula, but should you?
  - ✓ Breastfeeding, if possible, is the best way to give infants a good start emotionally and physically. Breastfeeding has health benefits for both mother and infant, promoting mother-infant bonding.
- You can limit juice and soda in your home, but should you?
  - ✓ Limit all added sugar your children consume to as little as possible. Just one 12-ounce can of soda has 12 teaspoons of added sugar, well above a child's maximum total daily intake of eight added teaspoons. Evidence is strong that the explosion of adult onset diabetes (type 2 diabetes) in both children and adults is directly linked to our high consumption of sugary drinks.
- You can regularly buy foods of convenience that are ultra-processed, but should you?
  - ✓ You should limit the amount of highly processed foods your children consume to as few as possible. They are likely to have access to plenty of this kind of food when they eat out, eat at friends homes, camps, and parties. We are just beginning to understand some of the health problems associated with consuming large amounts of processed food. Play it safe by limiting the processed food in your children's diet by providing as much whole food as possible.
- As a family, you can run through the fast food restaurants four or five times a week, but should you?
  - ✓ Most fast food is ultra-processed. You and your children should consume as little processed fast food as possible. A growing list of chronic

illnesses are linked to both nutritional excesses and deficiencies that result from consuming fast food.

- You can provide your children with a diet that nutrition experts recommend but should you make the effort?

  ✓ Eating a diet rich in fresh fruits and vegetables, whole grains, and lean protein is expensive and more time consuming to acquire and prepare than the typical American diet but probably well worth it. Current thinking is that a diet close to the Mediterranean diet is the healthiest available. From what we know today, every parent should try to maximize their children's fruit and vegetable consumption.

✓ The current medical consensus is that a traditional diet of whole foods rich in fruits and vegetables is best for children.

✓ Diets heavy in ultra-processed foods are associated with long-term health problems for three reasons:

- They contain too much sugar, artificial fat, and salt.

- They are deficient in some nutrients, most notably vitamin D and iron, as well as fiber.

- They arguably promote inflammation, asthma, and allergy in children.

✓ Current dietary practices in America seem to promote disease among our children.

✓ Experts believe that providing a diet rich in whole foods may prevent many of the diseases that commonly affect children and adults in America today.

✓ Providing a healthy diet for their children is one of the most important responsibilities parents have.

Paul Smolen, MD

CHAPTER THREE
Sphere #2: Screen Time

Allowing a screen in a child's room is akin to allowing the child to invite a stranger in for a sleepover.

Since the advent of films and television, parents have gradually lost some of their ability to control who is invited into their homes to talk to their children as well as the messages these outside influences bring. In our great grandparents' day, the only "outside the family" influences on children included church sermons, teachers at school, occasional visitors, and a handful of books, magazines, and newspapers. Religious activities and school were most children's main sources of contact outside their family's influence. In 1900 America, parents were masters of what surrounded their children. Today, in contrast, messages of all sorts can live in a child's bedroom 24/7, and his or her parent may or may not be aware of these. Screens bring the messages of all sorts of people with all sorts of motives and agendas. Some messages are healthy, but many try to sell them something or contain moral messages that parents might not condone. Some messages may expose children to violence, some may prey on or bully children, and many are just plain vulgar.

Screens of all sorts seem to be taking over our lives and especially the lives of our children. Currently, most school-aged children interact daily with TV commercial broadcast shows, computer educational material at school and at home, smart phones and tablets with interactive social media and gaming, and of course the ubiquitous video games. Everywhere a child turns today, a screen presents some kind of entertainment, social peer interaction, or informational content. To the extent possible, parents need to supervise and limit children's media interactions until they are old enough to make good decisions themselves. In order to help families make good screen decisions for their children, let's review what social scientists and health experts are recommending.

Why should parents care about their children's screen time?

Today's parents must know the potential effects of screen time on children and decide the rules for their Internet exploration. The most compelling reason to pay attention to how your children interact with screens is self-evident: time they spend in front of a screen is time they are not spending doing other activities like playing games, exploring outside, interacting with friends, reading, creating, solving disagreements with family and friends, learning how to be sensitive to others— in other words, learning the rules of social interaction that will be so crucial as they transition into adulthood. Time is a precious commodity for all of us, especially when that time is our childhood. Time is one of the few things we cannot buy more of, no matter how rich we are. One of a parent's major responsibilities is to help children make wise time management decisions throughout their childhood. Balancing a child's screen time with other activities is vitally important. Decisions about screen use are decisions that fall squarely into the can/should paradigm.

Most people would agree that the quality of anyone's life is directly related to the quality of the relationships we have with other people. Media and screens, while possibly educational, often isolate children. They generally provide solo activities that draw children away from direct human interaction. Loss of control of the messages, the isolation of a solo activity, and the loss of opportunity to play and learn from others are things parents need to keep in mind when drawing boundaries as far as screen time is concerned.

Information about screen time that all parents should know.

Parents need to have good information about the effect of screens on children before they confront the many decisions that screens bring into family life. Some of the current recommendations are based on data and studies, while some are merely opinion and speculation. In this chapter, I include only mainstream thinking on the subject of the influence of screen time on children. It goes without saying that, since every child is unique, the influence of particular screen content may be greater on one child than another child. Even though population studies cannot predict the influence of a particular screen event on an individual child, these studies still offer guidance for parents and pediatricians with regard to screens and children.

Let's start by defining what experts consider light, average, and heavy screen time for today's child. Consider this: on average, American children aged eight to eighteen years spend seven hours and eleven minutes in front of a screen daily.[36] Light use is considered up to three hours a day, whereas heavy screen time begins at 16 hours or greater a day. This heavy screen use is actually quite common, so common that it now has a name: "Internet/video game addiction disorder," or IAD.

The double-edged sword of screens.

Media exposure via screens can have both positive and negative effects on children. With a touch of a mouse or

---

[36]Rideout, V. J., U. G. Foehr, and D. F. Roberts. Generation M2: Media in the Lives of 8- to 18-Year-Olds. Menlo Park, CA: Kaiser Family Foundation, (2010).

button, children can watch performances of Tchaikovsky's ballet Swan Lake or experience a safari in the wilds of Africa. Television and the Internet have opened the world for almost every American child. A child can learn about nearly anything with these tools. He or she can pose questions and have them answered lightening fast and can gather information in seconds without ever needing to enter a physical library. Media experiences may include online tutoring interactions with people from different backgrounds and cultures. The educational opportunities of television and the Internet are limitless. Research suggests that television can be a positive influence on children when the programming is positive and viewing is planned, structured, and supervised.[37] Screens expand a child's world, and mastery of their uses may be vital to a child's ultimate educational and occupational success.

Unfortunately, a dark underside exists to electronic entertainment. Many parents are surprised to discover that children under age two can be harmed by television, even when it only plays in the background of family life and even when it is considered educational in nature.[38] One of the biggest challenges for a child under the age of two is to master language, and television and other screens can actually slow this process. We are not born speaking; we must learn language. Sorting through the myriad of vocabulary and language rules is a monumental task for anyone, especially for young children learning to walk, feed themselves, and follow rules all at the same time. Here is what experts have concluded about screens and very young children: generally speaking, children who have a lot of exposure to screen time have, on average, smaller vocabularies by age two.[39] Additionally,

---

[37]McCarthy, E. "Pediatricians and Television: It's Time to Rethink Our Messaging and Our Efforts." Pediatrics 131: 3 (March 1, 2013) 589-590.

[38]Brown A. "Media use by children younger than 2 years." Pediatrics 128:5 (November) 1040-5.

[39]Wright, J.C., A.C. Huston, K.C. Murphy, et al. "The relations of early television viewing to school readiness and vocabulary of children from low-in-

evidence does not support the use of "…educational media and educational TV…" marketed as giving very young children a head start toward literacy.[40] It actually may have the opposite effect, that of slowing language skills.[41]

The screen may be interesting and hold their attention, but meaningful learning may not occur.

Young children seem to learn language best from a loving, caring adult in a safe environment. Parents act as private language tutors for their children, teaching them things one-on-one. This method of teaching is far more effective than putting the one-way communication flow of a screen in front of them. Television is not interactive, and is thus not tailored to a child's language learning needs. Children are born to mimic, copy and learn. They are naturally curious, but their language skills may be so poor that they simply don't understand what the screen is showing them. The screen may be interesting and hold their attention, but meaningful learning may not occur. The parent's attention and example are more fun and effective at teaching language than a television screen no matter how colorful that screen may be. The Academy of Pediatrics statement about the effect of screens on young children is convincing with regard to turning off the television, even

---

come families: the early window project. <u>Child Development.</u> 2001:7 ( ).

[40]Media Use by Children Younger Than 2 Years, American Academy of Pediatrics Policy Statement. Pediatrics (October 17, 2011). <http://pediatrics.aappublications.org/content/early/2011/10/12/peds.201>1-1753.

[41]Zimmerman, F. J., D. A. Christakis, and A. N. Meltzoff. "Associations between Media Viewing and Language Development in Children Under Age 2 Years." <u>The Journal of Pediatrics</u> 151:4 (*date*) 364-368.

background television, as much as possible in the vicinity of children under two years of age.[42]

Media consumption also correlates with decreased academics and poorer language skills in older children.[43] The association is strong and documented repeatedly: the more television exposure a child has, the greater the chance of academic difficulties, and the smaller that child's vocabulary is likely to be.[44] [45] To be fair, it is possible that a child who has a lot of exposure to television may have an environment that is not conducive to good language skills; the television may have nothing to do with the child's slower language acquisition. No one knows the answer to this question. I believe that a child's access to television and other screens is simply a reflection of how much reading is going on in the home. More screen time means less conversation, reading, and storytelling time. Reading and story telling are active dynamic activities that stimulate a child's vocabulary and imagination in contrast to the passive, one-way flow of information from television images.

Why does a large amount of television viewing degrade a child's chance at academic success?

Television and other screen activities are generally passive, not active. Doing chemistry or mastering a foreign language uses much more mental power than passively watching television. Screens make children's brains lazy, incapable or unwilling to do the hard mental lifting required to master

---

[42]*See* "Media Use."

[43]Strasburger, Victor C., Amy B. Jordan, Ed Donnerstein. "Health Effects of Media on Children and Adolescents." Pediatrics 125: 4 (April 1, 2010) 756-767.

[44]*See* "Media Use."

[45]Wright, J.C., A. C. Huston, K. C. Murphy, M. St Peters, M. Pinon, R. Scantlin, J. Kotler. "The relations of early television viewing to school readiness and vocabulary of children from low-income families: the early window project." Child Development 72:5 (September-October 2001) 1347-66.

difficult school assignments. These are called home'work' and school'work' for good reason!

Sleep quality and duration is poorer around televisions, and with sleep impairment comes reduced cognitive ability.

In addition to making brains lazy, excessive screen time adversely affects sleeping. Strong evidence exists that screens in a child's room, especially television, impairs sleep. Sleep quality and duration is poorer around televisions, and with sleep impairment comes reduced cognitive ability. Bronson and Merryman's *Nurture Shock* provides an excellent discussion of the impact of a child having one hour less sleep a night.[46] In this book, the authors review recent studies looking at the effect of mild (one hour or less loss) sleep loss on a child's school performance. One study found that 30 minutes less sleep in the average sixth grader reduced performance to the level of the average fourth grader—a two-year impairment in intellect and social functioning. Another study demonstrated that loss of an hour's sleep lowers a child's score on a standard IQ test by seven points, as much as lead poisoning does! Learning new things requires sustained concentration and effort, seemingly the opposite of what screens offer.

Your child's brain is no different than any other body organ: the more it is exercised, the better it will work. Reading and stories at bedtime are exercise for their brains, enhancing a child's imagination, vocabulary, and ultimately his or her reading skills.[47] Households where parents provide lots of reading material, read to their children, and use sophisticated

---

[46]Bronson, Po and Ashley Merryman. Nuture Shock. New York: Twelve, 2009, Chapter 2.

[47]Smolen, Paul, M.D. "Bedtime Bliss for Everyone." DocSmo.com <http://www.docsmo.com/bedtime-bliss-for-everyone>. December, 2013, Episode 123.

language give their children a big heads up when it comes to school.[48]

Screens in their rooms interfere with the normal awake/sleep cycles that children so desperately need to thrive.

Screens in a child's room can mean big trouble with regard to sleep.

While parents may perceive that television has a calming effect on children, helping them to fall asleep, the evidence shows that the opposite is true: the more hours of television a child watches, the less likely it is that the child will sleep well. Using screens as part of the bedtime routine may impair children's ability to learn how to put themselves to sleep. Additionally, many researchers believe that the light coming from a screen inhibits the sleep process. Melatonin, a hormone that our brains produce at night in response to darkness, may not be produced under the influence of the blue light from screens. No matter what the mechanism of sleep disruption, the fact remains that many children become dependent on television and other screens to relax and lull them to sleep. This dependence is learned. Children are not born needing a screen to fall asleep. Too often parents facilitate this dependence. Establishing good sleep routines for children that do not include external devices is essential to teaching children to sleep well. Unfortunately, by age three years, 40% of American children have televisions in their rooms.[49] Whether to allow or even facilitate screens in a child's room is a major can/should decision for parents. The evidence is clear that allowing children to have screens in

---

[48]Trelease, Jim. The Read Aloud Handbook. New York: Penguin Books, 5th edition 2006.
[49]See Zimmerman.

their rooms interferes with the normal awake/sleep cycles that children so desperately need to thrive.

Screens invite strangers into your home.

Finally, screens invite strangers into our homes. Unless parents actively supervise and regulate the media content their children watch, some of the messages that come to them may include violence, degrading behavior and sexuality that is not appropriate for children. The average American child has witnessed 40,000 murders and 200,000 violent acts on TV by the time he or she graduates from high school.[50]

Much of the research that has been done since the invention of television has documented the fact that children often mimic what they see on television.[51] [52] Many researchers claim that television, unfiltered by parental commentary and input, can be destructive to a child's sense of right and wrong. It is naive to think that watching thousands of murders and violent acts on television and at the movies cannot have a deleterious effect on a young mind, especially one ill-equipped to interpret these messages. Increased aggression, increased impulsivity, ADHD behavior, and degrading attitudes toward others are just some of the problems that experts think are linked to the television or video game screen.

---

[50]Huston, A.C. et al. Big World, Small Screen: The Role of Television in American Society. Lincoln: University of Nebraska Press, 1992.

[51]Manganello, Jennifer A. and Catherine A. Taylor. "Television Exposure as a Risk Factor for Aggressive Behavior Among 3-Year-Old Children." Pediatrics and Adolescent Medicine, 163 (11): 1037 (2009).

[52]Ybarra et. al. "Linkages between internet and other media violence with seriously violent behavior by youth." Pediatrics. 122:5 (November 2008) 929-37.

Excess screen time may influence your child's health.

A close relationship exists between screen time and obesity.[53] [54] The use of screens is mostly a passive activity, requiring almost no energy output on the part of the child; a child can eat and participate at the same time. The distraction that a screen provides discourages portion control and encourages overeating. Moreover, the marketing messages coming from the screen most often promote the consumption of low quality food and beverages. Many governments around the world have noted this association between screen time and obesity in children and are talking action. The French, the Canadian, the Mexican, and now even the United States governments are taking action to curb the effect of marketing fast food, vending machine convenience foods, and sugary drinks on children.

Finding the right balance with regards to screen time.

When it comes to screens, video games, and media there are no simple answers for parents. Electronic media is, and will remain, part of our culture. Parents need to understand the effects, both positive and negative, that devices with screens have on their children. Messages and interactions children receive from screens have a major impact on their ultimate personality, intelligence, academic success, moral attitudes, and health. Somehow parents need to find a balance between the benefits and temptations that screens offer today's families.

---

[53]Ybarra et. al. "Linkages between internet and other media violence with seriously violent behavior by youth." Pediatrics. 122:5 (November 2008) 929-37.

[54]Ybarra et. al. "Linkages between internet and other media violence with seriously violent behavior by youth." Pediatrics. 122:5 (November 2008) 929-37.

Can/should screen decisions that parents need to make for their children:

Where should parents draw the line with regard to screen access? There is a spectrum that includes unfettered access to screens including in a child's bedroom at one end, and total avoidance of screens at the other end. Now that you are equipped with some of the basic facts, I want you to have a discussion, as a family, about where the right balance is for you and your children. Here are some of the questions I want you to discuss:

- Parents can include screen time for children two years of age and younger, but should they?
    - ✓ I recommend following the Academy of Pediatrics recommendation with regard to screens and young children. It recommends completely avoiding screen time, both active and passive watching, for children who are two years of age or younger. Researchers feel that even content marketed as "educational" and designed to enhance language skills in young children can slow down the language acquisition skills of children under two years of age. We know what is good for young children: reading, talking, responding to their language, showing them things, and interactive play. Parents are their child's best teacher—not a tablet or screen.

- Adults in the family can enjoy background television, but should they?
    - ✓ Background television slows the acquisition of language skills in children two years of age and younger. One of the big challenges very young children face is to master language. Experts recommend that parents enhance and speed up the learning of language by eliminating background television while children are awake. Responding to an infant and toddler's spontaneously generated language seems to be best. Reading to a child is one

37

of the most important things parents can do for their children.

- Parents can give children unlimited screen time, but should they?

  ✓ Experts recommend that children have no more than one or two hours of total screen time (television, computer, video games, and portable screens such as smart phones and tablets) per day. This recommendation is increasingly difficult to follow as screens become more portable and available; nonetheless, I think keeping it as a goal is useful. Here is a strategy I recommend to my patients with school age children: parents should enter into a contract with their children that forbids any non-educational screen time on Monday through Thursday—i.e., no television, video games, movies on tablets, and so forth. If the child abides by this rule and has a good week (defined however parents wish), then he or she may have unlimited screen time on a particular day or for an agreed portion of time during the weekend. The beauty of this strategy is that it forces a child to engage during the school week in other activities such as playing outside, reading, or being creative. What I often find is that when the weekend day comes with the "carte blanche" ticket to unlimited screens, the child would rather go play with his or her friends. This method devalues screens that children so covet. Moreover, in my experience most children will accept and abide by the school week screen ban if they are given one day of the week with unlimited screen time to enjoy. Under this arrangement, the child's total amount of screen time per week stays within the one to two hours per day limit recommended by the American Academy of Pediatrics, even if he or she choses to play video games for 14 hours on Saturday.

- Children can have various screens in their bedroom, but should they?
  - ✓ The evidence is strong that allowing screens in a child's bedroom is associated with poorer academic performance and sleep difficulties. Experts strongly discourage sleep rituals that involve television or other screens. In addition to interference with sleep and school performance, screens in children's bedrooms make it extremely difficult to limit their exposure to content that is not acceptable for them to view. Allowing Internet, texting, and media exposure in places where and when parents are not present and thus cannot oversee content can be dangerous. Parents should not invite strangers from screens into their child's bedroom.
- Parents can supervise children's viewing and electronic media activities, but should we?
  - ✓ Child development specialists agree that parents need to be active participants in their children's interaction with media, the Internet, and social media. Their active participation allows them to filter inappropriate content, limit total screen exposure time, help children interpret what they experience, and gives parents and children a chance to talk about these experiences from a caring adult's perspective.
- Many parents can afford to have a television in the dining room, but should they allow television viewing during meals?
  - ✓ The chance of children becoming obese increases if they spend too much time watching television. The correlation between screens and obesity is especially strong if children eat in front of a television and have unrestricted portions of food at the same time. Hence, experts strongly discourage eating while watching television. "Distracted eating" can lead to obesity in both children and

adults. Parents should turn off the television and talk to their children during meals. Not only will everyone have an easier time maintaining a healthy weight, but also parents will have the opportunity to share their values and observations.

✓ Screen time can have a strong and potentially negative impact on children.

✓ Research indicates the following potential negative effects of screen time on children:

- Slower language acquisition in young children
- Lower academic achievement
- Greater rates of obesity
- Higher rates of aggressive behavior
- Poorer sleep habits compared to peers

✓ Parents need to be savvy about how their children use screens, television, the Internet, social media, smart phones, and whatever is next!

CHAPTER FOUR
Sphere #3- Money

The fastest way for children to learn how to handle money is to let them handle money.

Twentieth century America witnessed an incredible rise in spending power for both parents and children. Historically, children had almost no disposable money to spend prior to the last century.[55] As their parents became more economically secure, children began to have the means to become purchasers in the marketplace.

Child labor laws undoubtedly added to the economic clout that children could achieve, both by restricting the amount of unpaid labor children could perform as well as codifying the concept of pay for work, even with relatively young children.

The twentieth century was financially rewarding for the average American family. Family income tripled, and, for the first time, children had the opportunity to become economic consumers—and did they ever start consuming! The following chart demonstrates family income:[56]

---

[55]United States. U.S. Department of Labor: 100 Years of U.S. Consumer Spending Washington: GPO, May 2006. <http://www.bls.gov/opub/uscs/report991.pdf>.

[56]*Caplow*, 164-165.

Average Annual U.S. Income of Middle-Income Families in 1999 Dollars Adjusted for Inflation

Year 1929	$15,745.00
Year 1959	$29,000.00
Year 1999	$47,809.00

By the end of the Twentieth Century, children had become an economic force of note. The following chart provides recent statistics about teen spending today:[57]

Teenage Consumer Spending Statistics

Total Number of U.S. Teens	25.6 Million
Total U.S. Teen Spending	$208.7 Billion
Total Annual Teen Income in U.S.	$91.1 Billion
Average Annual Income of 12-14 Year Olds	$2,167.00
Average Annual Income of 15-17 Year Olds	$4,023.00

Teens, and all children for that matter, are a force to reckon with in today's economy. Not only are they a significant group of consumers in the marketplace, but they also set the purchasing trends that the rest of us follow. Manufacturers of goods, especially clothing and electronics, pay close attention to the purchasing trends of children. An entire industry of clothing stores has been created to meet the needs of teens. Fast food restaurants lure children with toys, and the rest of the family follows. Restaurant profits have been enhanced by the economic power of three year olds... amazing!

Because families and children have more disposable income to spend, huge can/should dilemmas exist. Children's 'wants' and 'needs' have become blurred. Families are now making economic decisions that previously they did not face. The expression, "With ownership comes responsibility" is truer than ever: families now have more disposable income and therefore the responsibility to spend it wisely. For parents, spending on

---

[57]Marketingvox. "Rand Youth Poll." Seventeen, September 8, 2012. <http://www.statisticbrain.com/teenage-consumer-spending-statistics/>.

their children presents some difficult choices, such as: "How many of our child's wants do we satisfy?" "How do we avoid things like harmful video games and too much fast food?" "How does the family balance all of its financial obligations, including such things as the children's education and the parent's secure retirement?" Money opens up a lot of can and should questions!

To make matters worse, makers and retailers of food, clothing, toys, cereals and everything else imaginable have perfected the art of marketing to children.[58] They use likable cartoon characters, lure children toward products with promises of free toys, and buy powerful messages from role models such as athletes to remind children that their favorite celebrity is a consumer of whatever product is being marketed. Teaching children to decipher these marketing messages is a difficult but necessary part of good parenting.

Not only must today's parents contend with children's newfound economic freedom, but they must also find their own economic resources to raise their children. Although the average family's real income stopped rising in the 1980's, it remains at an all-time high level. Even though the purchasing power of families has plateaued, the cost of raising children has continued to rise. Current estimates are that the cost of raising the average American child born today will exceed $295,560 without the cost of college factored in![59] The College Board estimates that the current average cost of a four-year college degree from a public university is $91,304.00. For a private university degree, the cost jumps to $179,000.00.[60] To make matters worse, it is becoming increasingly difficult for children

---

[58]Shah, Anup. "Children as Consumers." Global Issues. 21 Nov. 2010. Web. 30 Sep. 2013. <http://www.globalissues.org/article/237/children-as-consumers>.

[59]Jyoti, Christine R. and Learn Vest. "Why it costs so much to raise a kid: The typical middle-income family will spend $235,000 raising a child to age 17. Here are some of the ways that cost adds up." <http://money.msn.com/family-money/why-it-costs-so-much-to-raise-a- kid>.

[60]College Board. <https://trends.collegeboard.org/home>.

to become financially independent; thus, adult children are living with their parents at rates not seen in decades.

Parents should set a goal to save fifteen percent of the family's gross income.

How can parents possibly meet all these challenges? The answer is that they must face the can/should decisions head on and make sound economic decisions when their children are very young. Planning for the entire family's future economic needs is the key. Parents must set priorities and carefully allocate family spending. With some planning and foresight, families may decide that a lot of the things that they can do may not be what they should do. We can buy a new car, hire a maid, eat out five times a week--but should we? Sound planning in the form of a family budget will give parents a sense of how much money is available to spend, while forcing them to make priorities for spending. In addition to spending, saving should be part of the budgeting process. Without a budget, spending tends to be impulsive and rise to the same level as a family's income or possibly beyond. Making a budget is the most important financial tool at a family's disposal. Parents should set a goal to save fifteen percent of the family's gross income. At this saving level, most families will be able to weather the ups and downs of financial life.

Wise financial decisions, such as keeping that older car a few more years, forgoing eating out a few times a week, or buying a little less for Junior can provide a child with much greater benefits if the money saved is set aside for such things as higher education, a down payment on a home, or a financial cushion going into adult life.[61] At a realistic six percent rate of return, $1000.00 set aside at a child's birth

---

[61]Smolen, Paul, M.D. "College Savings Made Easy." DocSmo.com, <http://www.docsmo.com/college-savings-made-easy-pedcast/>.

becomes $3,207.00 by the time the child is 20 years old, $4,292.00 at age 25 years and $5,743.00 by age 30 years.[62]

A family of four will save $1,456.00 per year if it reduces by two per week meals eaten at a fast food restaurant.[63] Invested, that sum becomes $56,689.00 in 20 years.

In addition to making decisions that benefit the family, parents who budget and save set an excellent example for their children. We know that children model behavior on the behavior of their parents: they are watching the way we make financial decisions and internalizing their own attitudes toward spending and saving. Social scientists provide strong evidence that adults who can live within their means and manage money well are happier in general with their lives.[64] Since all parents want their children to grow up to be happy, teaching them money management will contribute to their adult happiness. Here is a list of money management lessons that I suggest children master before they are adults:

- A child needs to understand that money is a limited resource and must be earned.

- A child must learn that when she chooses to buy one thing, she is precluded from buying something else.

- Children must learn the concept of saving for future spending and having a reserve fund for emergency spending needs.

- Children must learn the difference between spending for their needs and their wants.

---

[62]UltimateCalculators.com <http://www.ultimatecalculators.com/compound_interest_calculator.html>, <http://www.psychologytoday.com/blog/cant-buy- happiness/201301/what-is-happiness-five-characteristics-happy-people >.

[63]"Is Cooking Really Cheaper than Fast Food?" <http://www.mother-jones.com/tom-philpott/2011/10/cooking-really- cheaper-junk-food-mark-bittman>.

[64]Howell, Ryan T., Ph.D. Can't Buy Happiness? Money, personality, and well-being.

- When they are old enough to find work, children must balance their capacity to receive instantaneous (but low) paychecks with the long-term goal of academic success and much higher paychecks in the future.

- Children need to learn that giving to others is an important goal of money management.

Can/should questions for today's parents to ponder:

Here are some questions that I think parents should consider with regard to money and their children:

- Parents can make all the spending decisions for children, but should they? If so, at what age should children begin making decisions for themselves?

  ✓ By five years, most children have enough intuitive understanding of math to begin to make some purchasing decisions for themselves. By this age, most children have sufficient concept of money and numbers, to begin making transactions. Buying things on their own helps them learn about basic trade. Without the opportunity to handle money and make purchasing decisions for themselves, how will they ever learn to manage their own finances when they are adults?

- Parents can give children an allowance, but should they? If so, should parents require children to earn it?

  ✓ There is no clear answer here but I think the only way to learn to manage money and make good buying decisions is to practice. This presumes making good and bad decisions with money. I also think all children should be expected to help their families on a regular basis. I believe family help should not be in exchange for an allowance. I am not sure there is a right or wrong answer to the earning allowance question. I like to encourage helpfulness for the sake of helpfulness, not in exchange for money. See Chapter Five.

- Parents can give children extra money to save, but should they?
  - ✓ I would suggest and encourage savings but not force the issue. The power of savings will be obvious to most children over time. Saving is a habit that is slowly acquired by watching others. I think it is more important for parents to get into the habit of saving. Children will eventually imitate their parents' behavior. I think the overall philosophy to encourage is for children to take ownership and responsibility for their money. Only then will they begin to make good spending choices.

- Parents can direct their children's spending, but should they?
  - ✓ I recommend that parents interfere with a child's spending only when the purchase is either dangerous or out of bounds with their values and rules. Making some bad choices with money helps to teach a child the value of money. How will they learn to spend wisely if they don't ever experience "buyers remorse"?

- Parents can require their children to be responsible for their "needs" spending, but should they?
  - ✓ Allow me to describe to you the approach that one of my partners, Dr. Stephen Valder, took with his now almost adult children. I think Dr. Valder did a particularly good job of teaching money management to his children. As Dr. Valder says, "When they can count and understand numbers, they are ready to start learning money management."

Dr. Valder's example: he and his wife began giving their children an allowance of three dollars per week in kindergarten that they could use for snacks and toys. Dr. Valder and his wife expected their children to be helpful to the family at this age, but they did not require chores as a prerequisite to receiving their allowance. Their allowance was increased by one dollar per week for each year of school, so, by fifth grade, each child received eight dollars per week.

In the middle school years, their allowance increased to $10 per week in 6th grade, $12 per week in 7th grade, and $15 per week in 8th grade. With this increase in allowance came the new financial responsibilities of purchasing gifts for friends, purchasing their own music and entertainment, as well as any other wants they might have.

From sixth grade on, the Valders gave each child a $600 per year clothing allowance. Dr. Valder's children were forced to make real economic decisions with all the consequences attached to those decisions.

By high school, their weekly allowance increased to $20 per week from which all entertainment and transportation costs, gas and possibly car insurance had to be paid.

The Valders' plan provided a clear message from the beginning: the children had to be careful regarding how they spent their money because it was not unlimited. In the Valder household, children were forced to make financial decisions for themselves starting at a very young age. They got the idea that financial resources were limited, and they needed to spend wisely. This money management strategy also allowed parents to budget and save, only giving their children what they, the parents, could afford and not succumbing to their children's endless wants and desires. Dr. Valder's experience agrees with my observation that, "If you treat children like adults, they learn to act like adults."

- As a parent, parents can ignore the concept of saving, but should they?

  - ✓ I learned good financial decision making from my own family. My mother always made sure that I had a dime in my penny loafers in case of an emergency, but I understood that I should not spend that dime except for an emergency. When I started my own family, I quickly learned that our tendency was to spend all the money in our bank account if we left it there. The solution to that problem was to budget our spending and move the money out of our checking account as quickly as possible. It is now obvious that our children were watching, because they have adopted the same good financial decision making as adults. What you do has far more impact than what you say when it comes to children.

- Parents can put their children's financial needs and wants above their own, but should they?

  - ✓ I'll never forget a conversation I had with a fellow doctor in my hometown who sent four children to an expensive private school all the way through high school. He had spent hundreds of thousands of dollars on his children's educations, and they hadn't even gone to college yet! He regretted that he had not saved for their college educations, nor had he adequately funded his own retirement. He had made the financial mistake of putting his children's short term needs above the family's long-term needs. In the rearview mirror of life, he could see that he had made a large error.

✓ Children today are major consumers in our economy.

✓ Helping children learn to manage their money is vital to their ultimate happiness.

✓ Some of the major money lessons children need to learn include:

- Money is limited and must be earned.

- Saving a portion of one's money is important.

- Needs are different than wants.

✓ Parents have the difficult task of balancing what they can provide their children and what they should provide.

CHAPTER FIVE
Sphere #4 Family Responsibility

**Life for children has changed drastically
in the past 100 years.**

hildren born in the year 1900 were valuable sources of labor for their families and communities. We have all seen photographs of children working in large industrialized plants making clothing or other textile items. Their childhoods were a far cry from the experience of most children in Western countries in the year 2015. In 1900, children entered the adult world of work, demands, deadlines, and stress long before they ever had a chance to develop their own interests, intellect, or talents.

**Children who are taught to enjoy work
are given a great gift.**

Even the school calendar was created to accommodate the work children could do on farm. Their help was essential to the financial viability of the family. Children, lots of them, were an important force underpinning an economically viable family. They were often the difference between economic security for a family and desperate poverty. Children had to learn to complete work and thereby produce income quickly, or they were a burden to their families. Think of the skills they had to master at very young ages. By elementary age, male children were likely skilled with firearms, hunting, fishing, handling and care of domestic farm animals, basic mechanical repair, tending crops, and use of farm machinery; moreover, they were capable of working outside the home in places such as mines and factories. Similarly, female children likely could cook, preserve food by canning, repair and make clothes, care for siblings and the elderly, and work outside the home in places such as factories.

In many families, children growing up in America in the 21st century have little or no responsibility to contribute toward a family's well being. Every parent needs to confront the issue of how much to expect children of various ages to contribute in terms of family chores, caretaking of relatives, and finances. To a large degree, these are personal decisions, but some guidance may be useful.

Although I am not advocating returning to the harsh days of our great-great grandparents, we do need to find the sweet spot when it comes to making demands on our children. We are back to those can/should decisions. We can let our children have a childhood devoid of significant family chores and responsibilities, but should we? How much should we expect of our children, and at what age(s)? Moreover, how do we balance all the other demands made on today's children?

An attitude of helpfulness needs to be cultivated.

Parents are the captains of the USS Family. They are the Steven Spielbergs of their children's youth, directing the script that these children will someday call their childhood. Parents possess so much control over the decisions that determine children's formative experiences: where their children live, where they go to school, whether or not they participate in religious experiences, whether they learn to swim, how many siblings they have, and to a large degree, their attitude toward themselves and others.

Parents are also the architects of what experts call the "emotional climate" in which a child is raised.[65] The American Academy of Pediatrics (AAP) is beginning to recognize the importance to childrearing of an emotionally healthy household. The AAP created a task force to describe and define an "emotionally healthy environment" in order to help pediatricians guide families toward the formation of such environments for children. The AAP experts believe that parents who have a healthy attitude about life and create healthy "emotional climates" for their children have a much easier time raising successful children than parents who display excessive negativity, self doubt, or anger.

Parents are the most important teachers children will ever have. Thus, the effect of their attitudes toward children and life in general is powerful. Parents want the best for their children. I also believe it is axiomatic that every family is unique. Every family is defined by its own blend of strengths and weaknesses—the strengths and weaknesses of its members. Each family member has a unique personality. Mix those personalities into family groups, and the result is that each family has its own way of communicating, interacting, and parenting. Successful families share some common features that help create success in the children they produce.

Neuropsychologist Dr. John Medina summarized current psychological research on the subject of parenting and child success in his book *Brain Rules for Babies*. He concludes that the best outcomes for children are produced when parents are "demanding but warm."[66] Dr. Medina describes the "demanding and warm" parents as follows:

---

[65]"Report of the Task Force on the Family." Pediatrics 111: 2 (June 1, 2003). <http://pediatrics.aappublications.org/content/111/Supplement_2/1541.full?sid=4197c8ae-2eb4-4730-8f6e-ae458d95d7d>.

[66]Medina, John. *Brain Rules for Babies*. New York: Pear Press (2010), 361-367.

- Having high, but age appropriate, expectations for their children.

- Encouraging independence in their children.

- Emotionally engaged with their children's behavior and feelings through listening and empathizing.

- Effectively communicating their expectations without being too authoritarian or rigid.

- Being able to help their children understand and interpret the emotions of others and themselves by offering them a mature adult perspective.

Successful parents are relatively strict and expect their children to achieve success at school and with peers, all in an environment that shows love and respect for the child's individuality. Parents of successful children probably do not praise children simply to improve self-esteem. Such parents probably expect their children to perform meaningful, age-appropriate chores throughout their childhood and they follow through with negative consequences when their children fail to meet reasonable expectations.

Po Bronson and Ashley Merryman come to the same conclusions in their book, *Nurture Shock*.[67] After analyzing the current research regarding the reinforcing of self-esteem and households saturated with parental praise, they conclude that the net effect of all this "you are great" talk is to put too much pressure on children—to make children's expectations of themselves unrealistic and negative—the exact opposite of what their parents intended. These authors also concluded that some criticism of children, when done in a loving way, improves overall performance on tasks and that children who are allowed to fail at things once in a while are ultimately more persistent and successful at achieving their life goals. The old saying "failure is the best teacher" is really true, and

---

[67] *See* Bronson.

excessive praise of children simply insulates them from their own failures. Families that create an emotional climate that is both demanding and warm seem to raise the most successful and happy children.

Benefits of a responsible attitude in your child:

Surprisingly, I could find little research on how a child benefits from affirmatively contributing to the family's well being. To analyze this issue, we have to use common sense. A child's first response to a parent's assignment of a chore is to resist. This response is only natural. Few people accept new work and new responsibilities without some resistance. Time and patience, however, will likely cure negative attitudes.

If parents willingly and freely give of themselves to make sure the family functions well, I believe their children will eventually adopt the same attitude.

How do parents instill in their children an enjoyment of work and a willingness to be helpful to one's family and community? Parents consciously or unconsciously teach these attitudes to their children by example. Children learn attitudes toward work and acceptance of responsibility by imitation. If parents enjoy work and find it meaningful, their children probably will as well. If parents willingly and freely give of themselves to make sure the family functions well, I believe their children will eventually adopt the same attitude. With time and patience, when the family says, "We need you to do this or that," a child will hear, "They need me." When the family says, "We expect you to do this or that," a child will eventually hear "They count on me." When a family asks, "Will you help us do this or that," a child feels competent, important, and needed. Children like to be needed. Initial resistance and resentment will, with time and patience, turn into pride, confidence, and a spirit of cooperation. Incorporating children into the work routines of a family is a first exposure to work. Positive experiences within the family will lead to positive experiences beyond the family in school and work.

We all know that learning to enjoy one's work is one of the keys to a happy life. Work and service to others are parts of the formula for a satisfying and meaningful life. Forgetting or procrastinating chores has different consequences when judged by our families than when an employer makes the call. These lessons need to be learned early in the context of a safe "demanding but warm" environment. Success and failure is our best instructor when it comes to behavior.

A persistent parent can teach children these valuable lessons before they reach adulthood. Here are some of the opportunities relating to chores and family helpfulness that children have to learn:

- Work is important and rewarding in itself.
- Failure to follow through with duties has consequences for the child and also for others who rely on the child.
- Accepting responsibility for failures is essential to gaining the trust of others.
- Doing a job well is satisfying.
- Mastering new skills can be fun and empowering.
- Trust and respect for others are some of the most important things we can learn.
- Work provides a sense of gratitude for the contributions of those around us.

There is a line where family responsibilities cease to be useful to children and become an onerous burden; this line is different for different families, and it needs to be drawn with the individual child's life circumstances in mind. Generally speaking, if household chores add too much stress for a child, it is time to reduce them. If the chores are interfering with a healthy amount of free time to spend with friends and family, again, it's time to reduce them. If the chores are creating a lot of conflict between parents and children, parents need to lower the demands and reevaluate the number of chores, the maturity level of their child, and the emotional context in which the family is communicating or not communicating.

A sample list of age appropriate chores:

At what age should parents begin asking children to accept household responsibilities? What are age-appropriate tasks that we should expect from our children? The answers to these questions are different for different families. Generally, as soon as a child is old enough to understand language, he or she is old enough to help with family chores. Here are my suggestions for chores for children of various ages.

Chores for children ages 2 to 4

- Pick up debris in the yard.
- Put toys away.
- Feed a pet.
- Bring things to parents on request.
- Pile books and magazines.

Chores for children ages 4 to 6

Any of the above chores, plus:

- Carry dirty dishes to the sink.
- Help with yard chores.
- Help with laundry.
- Gather dirty clothes.
- Help with weeds in garden and flowerbeds.
- Water plants outside.

Chores for children ages 6 to 10

Any of the above chores, plus:

- Dust.
- Vacuum.
- Help with yard work and gardening.
- Set the table and help with cleanup.
- Carry and put groceries away.
- Care for a pet by feeding, walking, or grooming.
- Sort laundry.

Chores for children ages 10 and older

Any of the above chores, plus:

- Yard work including grass cutting and carrying debris.
- Weeding, watering, and planting.
- Car cleaning.
- Pet care.
- Fold and distribute laundry.
- Vacuum, dust, and straighten.
- Make one's bed.
- Clean bathrooms.

In my family, we modified the above list to suit our children's individual personalities. As a young teen, our daughter showed interest in gardening and cutting grass. She quickly mastered the use of a gas-powered mower, mulching flowerbeds, and tending a vegetable garden. I think it is no accident that as a young adult, she is a very competent gardener and cook. She has been able to parlay skills that she learned doing family chores into adult hobbies and talents. Our son, on the other hand, enjoyed helping me pay bills and complete woodworking projects. As an adult, he is now a competent wood craftsman as well as an adroit manager of his own hard-earned money. Those family chores we initiated taught important life skills to both of our children.

Should an allowance be linked to chores?

Many parents struggle with the concept of an allowance for their children. We have already discussed this in detail in Chapter Four. I don't think there is a right or wrong answer to whether linking allowance to chores is beneficial to a child. The essential question is this: you can give your children money for completing household responsibilities and chores but should you? Should children earn money for the chores they do around the house? Additionally, is there a level of effort and work asked of children where they should be paid? These questions have different answers for different families and children. One approach that I recommend is as follows:

- **Allowance**: A basic allowance, beginning when children are old enough to understand how to count money, is reasonable and is a valuable learning tool for them. Money in their pockets teaches them how to save and how to make judgments about spending money. Having to spend limited resources for items of little pleasure teaches invaluable lessons to children. Over time, they will learn to assess their wants more carefully by making their own spending decisions. If it's their money, they will learn how to maximize the value of it. No one is more careful with money than the *owner*. An allowance facilitates that lesson.

- **Chores**: My opinion is that parents should not link chores to allowance, but rather to the child earning privileges such as participation in family game night, sleepovers with friends, screen time, or a special outing with a parent. Other experts agree with this approach.[68] [69] I like an allowance that is not conditioned upon the success or failure of completing chores; such an allowance gives a child a small amount of money with which to learn spending and saving lessons.

- **Savings**: Rather than requiring children to save a portion of their allowances, I think that they should be encouraged to save. At some point, the concept of saving and charity should be introduced.

Can/should questions for parents:

- Parents can ask their children to do chores, but should they?

  ✓ It's hard for me to think of a situation where a parent would not want to require children to contribute labor and energy to the well being of the family. Even most handicaps do not preclude all tasks. On rare occasions, a child may be so physically or mentally handicapped that completing family responsibilities is impossible. Except in these cases, I think that all children should be expected to be helpful members of their families, and parents should encourage and insist that they are.

- At what age can children begin chores, and at what age should they begin?

  ✓ Parents should enlist children's help as soon as they are old enough to understand language. Even very small children can help pick up toys. Young children often have a desire to learn to do things

---

[68]"Kids and money." CNN Money Online, Lesson 12, 2014. <http://money.cnn.com/magazines/moneymag/money101/lesson12/i ndex5.htm>.

[69]"Allowance Tips: Good Money Management Begins with an Allowance." National PTA Family Education Staff. <http://life.familyeducation.com/allowance/parenting/36441.html#ixzz2gcJ0hT5t>.

for themselves; cultivate this urge starting at a young age. It will serve them well as they get older.

- You can afford to pay your children for chores, but should you?

  - ✓ In my opinion, parents should pay for chores only when older teens perform them and only when the chores are beyond their normal duties. If an older child expends a large amount of effort and energy on a special task at a parent's request, it is reasonable but not essential to compensate the child beyond his or her usual allowance. See the discussion in Chapter Four.

- You can praise a child's strong effort at a task, or you can praise his or her accomplishment—which should it be?

  - ✓ I think that parents should praise effort, not just accomplishment. Hard work trumps almost everything when it comes to success in life. Besides, reward without effort is unnatural. Success without hard work doesn't happen much in life, and when children achieve consistent success (praise) without much effort, they are likely not to have much grit or determination when they do ultimately fail at something. This principle of praising effort over achievement is just as relevant to a child learning to take on family responsibility as it is for them to master school work, a sporting skill, or job skills.

- You can reward helpfulness in many ways, but how should you?

  - ✓ A parent's approval and praise are the best rewards they can give. Parents' approval or disapproval is their most powerful tool to motivate children. The ultimate reward for a child is the parent's love, acceptance, and praise.

- You can do the work faster and easier than your children; why should you make the effort to involve them?

  ✓ Work gives life meaning and purpose. As children progress from total dependency to self-sufficiency, they must learn a lot of small skills that parents teach them. Children love to learn new things and are naturally curious. Parents should take advantage of these traits by teaching them every skill possible, from cooking to carpentry. Not only will they benefit, but also parents will eventually obtain more help and free time for themselves. The short-term loss in efficiency will eventually reap its rewards with a skilled child. Additionally, the self-sufficient child will feel good about himself and begin to appreciate the labor and talents of others.

✓ Teaching children to find meaningful work is one of the most important parenting tasks.

✓ Parents who "demand" that their children achieve success in childhood tasks, but at the same time are "warm and responsive" to their emotional needs tend to have the most successful children.

✓ Excessive praise is damaging to children.

✓ Giving age-appropriate chores to children is good for their emotional development and self esteem.

✓ Paying children for chores is a matter of individual family choice.

CHAPTER SIX
Sphere #5 Academics, Extracurricular, and Unstructured Play

The new time equation for children in the 21st century America.

Various sociological factors have come together in the 21st century to make finding the balance between school, extracurricular activities, and free time more difficult than in previous generations.

As we saw in Chapter One, family size today is dramatically smaller, on average, than a hundred years ago, allowing parents to invest far more energy, time, and money into each child's education and activities. Additionally, most children have far fewer work and family obligations than the children who preceded them; they have more disposable time.

Most children in modern Western countries no longer live on farms, perform manual labor, or care for younger siblings. These factors, along with ever-increasing academic pressures, have given children more free time to fill as they choose while requiring less physical work and fewer family responsibilities. Moreover, families have more money to invest in extracurricular activities. The balance of work, school, and play today has far more permutations than it did in years past.

Many parents can and do push to get their children to the top of whatever activity they desire such as athletics, academic achievement, or performance in the arts…but at what cost? How hard should parents push, and how do they know if they have pushed too hard? A child's time and attention are not unlimited, and spending large amounts of time learning to play ice hockey, for instance, leaves less time for other things. Are there costs to pursuing goals for children's achievement? Yes, and I contend that sometimes the costs can be too high. Finding the right balance between academic activities, extracurricular pursuits, and free play is an important task for every parent. I hope that the following discussion will help parents to make the best decisions for their families with respect to balancing the precious time of childhood.

Parents need to provide opportunities for their children, not resumes.

In addition to smaller family sizes, increased financial resources, and more free time, the modern information age is another factor in the quest for parents to have their children excel in academics, sports, music, and just about everything else. Many parents begin building resumes for their children before they are able to climb the ladder on the slide at the playground.

We have all heard of parents competing to get their children into the "right preschool." For some parents, the path to power and ultimate success for their children is clear, and they want to set children on this path a very young age. Many parents see themselves as the makers and managers of their children's resume and ultimate career. They know that people with college degrees have an economic edge in our society. Our society values education and knowledge over manual and technical skills and services. Based on 2010 numbers from the United States Census Bureau, here are the relative economic values of various levels of education compared to having a high school degree only:

Educational Degree	Earnings[70]
High School	X=High School Graduates Income
Some college without completion	1.18X
Associates Degree	1.28X
Bachelor Degree	1.66X
Master Degree	2.6X
Professional Degree	3.25X
PhD	3.20X

It is obvious why parents become so invested and engaged in their children's schoolwork: success in the classroom for most students translates into increased earning power in their futures. This degree of income advantage holds true every year for the person's working life. Education seems to be the golden ticket to financial success.

Parents rightfully want the best for their children. Unfortunately, sometimes they are driven to do some strange hyper-parenting. Psychologist David Elkind noticed something happening to childhood back in the early 1980s that he describes in his classic book, *The Hurried Child.*[71] Dr. Elkind felt that parents' emphasis on skill acquisition and academics was fundamentally changing childhood by altering the time that children had traditionally used for unstructured play.. I think that Dr. Elkind noticed the beginning of a trend that has only intensified since his original observations back in the 1980's.

In the minds of many parents today, the formula is simple: academic success = financial success = adult happiness. I do no think that the evidence validates this formula. In the Grant Study or The Harvard Study of Adult Development, since 1938 investigators have been collecting detailed information

---

[70]United States. Census Bureau. Washington: GPO, 2010.

[71]Vaillant, George. Triumphs of Experience. Boston: Harvard, 2012.

about a group of men who attended Harvard between 1939-1944.[72] The researchers sought to discover what factors created a good life for these men as they aged. They have collected data on these subjects until they reached the age of 80 years.

The investigators carrying out the Harvard Grant Study wanted to find out how this cohort of men changed over their lives, what they valued as they aged, and what about their lives made them happy and fulfilled. Dr. Vaillant, a psychiatrist who led the study in recent years, has documented how destructive alcohol and tobacco are to one's physical health. Those participants who drank and smoked heavily frequently suffered premature death and illness. The study also noticed that alcoholism correlates strongly with divorce. Mental illness occurs far more often among the men who smoked and drank heavily than among those who did not.

Interestingly, the data did not support the correlation of a superior IQ with greater success or wealth among the study participants. Most important are the conclusions the study drew from the happiness data. Here the conclusions were clear: happiness in these men was directly related to the "warmth" and quality of the relationships they were able to develop both with their parents, friends and family. As principal researcher Dr. Vaillant put it, "Happiness is love, full stop." If we develop the ability to love those around us, we are likely to find happiness. From this observation, we can extrapolate that the level of emotional engagement we cultivate in our children can reap great rewards for them as they mature. We all need and seek unconditional love, and this is true for our children as well. An elite education gives

---

[72]Vaillant, George. Triumphs of Experience. Boston: Harvard, 2012.

children a major advantage and opportunity in life, but, by itself, it does not bring happiness by itself, pure and simple.

How do parents create children who are destined to become happy adults?

Finding and cultivating children's talents is just one of a parent's jobs; parents are also responsible for helping children achieve balance among the many aspects of their lives. When it comes to personality traits, the term "balanced" refers to an equal mixture of abilities in three main childhood domains: mastering academic school work, cultivating extracurricular (outside of schoolwork) interests, and learning vital social-interpersonal skills. I think we can all agree that being a balanced child or adult is a good thing; balanced children are usually destined for success and happiness as adults. Parents need to foster as much balance in children as possible, taking into account each child's natural temperament, intelligence, and talents. Helping children find "balance" in their personality is vital for personal growth and development.

What's the right mix of activities for my child?

What do experts recommend is the right mix of these three activities? It depends on a child's interests, talents, temperament, and persistence. Very few parents are tasked with the challenge of raising a Mozart or Shakespeare, undoubtedly children who possessed true genius intellects. Most of us are destined to have children who are funny, unique, witty, and loving, but who possess more ordinary gifts. We, as parents, want to offer the best to our children, but what *is* the best? Someday, if we are lucky, we will send our children off into the world confident, secure, educated, and having enough self-sufficiency to take care of themselves and those around them. Hopefully, by the time they reach the age of independence, our children will have a strong sense of their own interests and talents. This sense is nurtured by encouragement, fertilized by our interest in the child's unique talents, and unleashed when we provide opportunities for them to try a range of activities throughout childhood. Exposing children to a wide variety of academic and extracurricular interests is one of the great joys of being a parent; watching them discover, explore, and possibly master and surpass our own expertise is an awesome experience, one that all parents should have.

While balance is the key to raising a successful child, forcing 'balance' through a slew of weekly activities runs the risk of spreading a child's energies too thin. Recent research has found that middle and high school aged children who participate in extracurricular activities can both benefit from and be harmed by these activities.[73] Generally the effects of such activities are beneficial, but when finding time to do schoolwork becomes difficult, the time conflict may pose a serious problem for children. Anyone who has played a high school sport knows about the difficulty of completing homework while traveling, playing, and recovering from the day's competition. Any extracurricular activity presents similar challenges.

It is fun to have big dreams, but parents need to be realistic and set realistic goals for their children.

How often do childhood interests turn into a career?

The following chart provides some sobering statistics about a child's chances of turning sports participation into a lifetime career. Earning a living from sports is obviously a very different challenge than mastering skills on the field, court, or ice. Only a tiny percentage of athletes that achieve success at

---

[73]Fredricks, Jennifer A. and Jacquelynne S. Eccles. "Is extracurricular participation associated with beneficial outcomes? Concurrent and longitudinal relations." Developmental Psychology 42:4 (Jul 2006): 698-713.

the college level ultimately enjoy professional athlete status after graduation. [74]

Chance of a Child Becoming a Professional Athlete

Sport	High School Level Player	College Level Player
Men's Baseball	11.6%	0.6%
Men's Football	1.7%	0.08%
Men's Soccer	1.0%	0.04%
Men's Ice Hockey	1.3%	0.01%
Women's Soccer	0.9%	0.03%

It is fun to have big dreams, but parents need to be realistic and set realistic goals for their children.

Is unstructured play valuable for children or a waste of their time?

Extracurricular activities are, by definition, structured events that act as extensions of a child's school environment. While they can provide invaluable contributions to a child's development, they need to be balanced with unstructured playtime. Experts at the Academy of Pediatrics recommend a healthy dose of "child driven" play to help a child develop creativity, endurance, strength, social and cognitive skills, as well as simply to have fun.[75]

Play allows children to use their creativity while developing their imagination, dexterity, and physical, cognitive, and emotional strength. Play is important to healthy brain development: through play children engage and interact in the world around them at an early age. Play allows children to create and explore a world they can master, conquering their

---

[74]"NCAA Statistics." Business Insider. Feb. 2012. <http://www.businessinsider.com/odds-college-athletes-become-professionals-2012-2?op=1>.

[75]Ginsburg K. "The Importance of Play in Promoting Healthy Child Development and maintaining Strong Parent-Child Bonds." Pediatrics 119: 1 (January 2007): 183.

fears while practicing adult roles, sometimes in conjunction with other children or adult caregivers…As they master their world, play helps children develop new competencies that lead to enhanced confidence and the resiliency they will need to face future challenges.

Parents often think of this free playtime as wasted, but experts have a different opinion.

This author adds that unstructured play driven by children, not adults, offers children a chance to develop themselves physically, solve problems as they arise, learn leadership skills, and gain experience in managing the dynamics of a group. In other words, experts are recommending we return to what seems to be missing so often in children's lives today: unstructured, unsupervised play with other children—play for the sake of play. Parents often think of this free playtime as wasted, but experts have a different opinion. They see it as vital to a child's psychosocial development.

As you can probably tell by now, my idea of the optimal work/play balance for children falls somewhere between the extremes of total scheduling and all of a child's time being spent in unstructured play. I recommend providing children with plenty of opportunities to grow in all aspects of their development. Finding the balance for each individual child is key. It is your obligation to insist that your children do their best in school, develop physically, master basic social skills, and broaden themselves with a generous dose and variety of extracurricular activities.

Fast is not necessarily best.

Finally, I'd like to refer you back to the work of David Elkind, the professor who identified the "hurried child," a product of what he termed "hyper-parenting". For Dr.

Elkind, parents who micromanage their children's lives and have unrealistic expectations of their children cause them stress. He felt this type of parenting is quite destructive for children. Dr. Elkind felt that children in these families are being robbed of their childhood and often do not master all the developmental tasks that children need to become strong, resilient, well-balanced adults. He also felt that the "hurrying" could stifle a child's creativity—one of the most important personality traits that make us human and unique individuals. Here is a very partial list of how Dr. Elkind feels we "hurry" today's child:

- By promoting "earlier is better" philosophy
- By encouraging children to adapt to "adult schedules"
- By exaggerating the "dangers of outside" and by bringing "childhood inside"
- By over emphasizing "academic success"
- By encouraging children to become "miniature adults"[76]

What are the signs that my child is under too much pressure?

Every child is an individual and may react to stress in his or her own, unique fashion. Common symptoms however, usually allow parents to identify stress in their child. Being aware of these stress reaction symptoms is vital to recognizing when a child is experiencing excessive stress. The most common symptoms in stressed children include sleep disturbances, bodily complaints like headache and stomachache, and fatigue over an extended period of time. Additionally, easy crying, overly aggressive or immature behavior, tics, skin picking, and difficulty with separation from parents are also usually symptoms of a stressed child. Parents should always be alert to these symptoms in their children.

---

[76]Elkind, Chapter 2.

If they recognize any of them, they should seek help from their child's pediatrician and examine how they can lower the emotional temperature for their child.

What has this pediatrician witnessed in the past generation?

My own experiences with thousands of families have provided me with a front row perspective regarding many of the issues that Dr. Elkind raises. In my thirty-two years of pediatric practice, I have observed five family archetypes:

- In the first archetype, the parents are successful and hard driving. Often, one of the parents reached a fairly high level of success in athletics as a child and wants his or her children to have equal or greater success. This parent invests a large amount of emotional energy, time, and money in lessons, equipment, travel, and training camps for the child or children. All of this family's extra time, money, and energy seem to be invested in their children's achievement. The children's unstructured playtime and social skills often suffer in this scenario. I have seen families achieve some success from their intense focus on skill acquisition over the years, but generally I have seen a lot of disappointment and unhappiness occur in these families. This unhappiness stems from a sense of failure by both the children and the parents. The parents set expectations high—probably too high—from the outset. Ironically, I have never seen any superstar athletes produced from this type of family. I think this family's desire to produce a superstar athlete or performer has caused them to sacrifice some of their children's free unstructured play—for little long-term gain.

- The second family archetype is similar in some respects to the first, but in a different way: instead of spending large amounts of money and time training their child for a particular skill, this family minimizes children's needs for education and social interaction by putting them into the working world at a very young age. A family business such as a farm or small business becomes the place where these children spend much of their childhood. Sacrificing academics, extracurricular activities, and free play doesn't seem to work very well. The "work in your free time" model tends to breed resentment toward their parents on the part of the children involved and can stifle the children's education.

- The third family archetype is what Dr. Elkind calls the "prodigy parents," those who believe that no school or activity is good enough for their children. I have seen a number of families who have literally moved their children from school to school because the schools failed to perceive the special gifts of their children. These parents had great difficulty accepting average as an adjective for their children. Their children's failures were always a problem created by others, be it their school, their friends, or whatever structured activity they were participating in. There was just no school good enough for their children. Parents in these families believe that other adults simply cannot recognize their children's greatness. This attitude puts tremendous pressure on children, since the parents have set expectations extremely high and the children's achievement is likely to fall short of what these parents expect. My experiences tell me that families who follow this model of parenting often have children who exhibit major rebellion and destructive behavior when the teen years arrive.

- The fourth family archetype is one that I am seeing more and more. These are usually families with great means who have extremely high expectations for their children academically and hope that they will get the edge by getting an "elite" education and a top notch career. These families choose prestigious boarding schools that are usually many hundreds or thousands of miles away from their families, in the hopes that this type of education will give their children a leg up on admission to an Ivy League school. These families are willing to give up their day-to-day influence on their children in the name of academic and life success.

- The fifth family archetype is one that I see often. In this family, both parents work long hours and consequently depend on daycare, babysitters, and media devices to entertain their children. They have a reasonable income but are often exhausted from earning it. Their children often lack opportunities to make friendships and are deprived of unstructured playtime with other children. These parents are often very generous to their children, providing them with the newest video games, computers, TVs, and electronics in their bedrooms. Academic expectations for these children tend to be low and these low expectations are reflected in the children's achievement. Lack of time is these parent's worst enemy. This lack of time does not permit them to allow their children to participate in many extracurricular activities. Children in this type of family are losing out on all fronts: academics, extracurricular opportunities, and unstructured free play.

How do families find the correct balance?

So, what is the right mix for your family? How does your family find the right balance of academics, extracurricular activities, and unstructured free play? I offer the following guidelines:

✓ Children should be afforded an hour of unstructured play for every hour of structured activities they participate in.

✓ One or two extracurricular activities at a time are enough.

✓ Families should not sacrifice their own financial security in hopes that a child will be able to cash in on a skill learned during childhood.

✓ Sports should be rotated throughout the year to minimize overuse injuries as well as burnout.

✓ If a child complains of being tired a lot or seems anxious, she may need more unstructured play.

✓ Provide the best education you can, making sure that this education does not overwhelm your children with work and does not stifle their love of learning and creativity.

✓ The most important teachers in a child's life are her parents. Create an atmosphere of curiosity in your home; it is infectious.

✓ Reading to your children all through childhood is the most important thing you as a parent can do to ensure their academic success.

✓ Limit screens and screen time, especially in your child's room.

✓ Don't get overly involved in your children's schoolwork. Your children will abdicate responsibility for their own work.

We as a family can invest all of our free time and energy into these activities, but should we? Here are some can/should questions I would like you to consider:

• Families can provide opportunities for extracurricular activities for children but should they? If so, how many activities are right for children in elementary, middle, and high school?

✓ The answer to this question really depends on the particular child's interests. I recommend that when children are in elementary and middle school, parents should allocate an equal amount of time to after school academics, extracurriculars, and free unstructured play. Evidence supports limiting extracurricular activities to no more than two activities at a time in high school. Regardless of their ages, parents should be sensitive to the signs of stress in their children. Should these signs appear, parents should assess why their children are stressed and take steps to address this problem.

- Parents can make unstructured play a priority for their children, but should they?

✓ Yes. Unstructured play is not a waste of time. In fact, it seems to be vital to a child's physical and emotional wellbeing and development. Playground experiences allow children to solve problems with one another, be physically active, learn group cooperation skills, and develop close emotional attachments with friends. Families should make unstructured play time a priority for their children.

- Parents can facilitate children focusing on one activity year-round, but should they?

✓ No, except under unusual circumstances. Childhood is a time to explore many facets of one's personality and develop likes and dislikes. Trying a range of activities is essential to that process. Additionally, concentrating on one sport year-round frequently leads to overuse injuries. Skeletally immature children, generally those under the age of 16, need to get various types of exercise so as to not overuse limited groups of muscles.

- Parents can decide the quantity and specifics of children's extracurricular activities, supplemental academic experiences, and friendships, but should they be the sole decision makers?

✓ The answer to this question boils down to opinion, observation, and common sense. Children need to develop all facets of their personality: cognitive competence, specialized skills, physical stamina and agility. They also need to master interpersonal communication. In order to accomplish these tasks, they need to be fully engaged emotionally. A parent's role is to provide opportunities, structure, and guidance in the process of activity selection, but the child, when old enough, should decide on the specifics of the activity. For example, one of the major goals for parents is to keep children physically active. Thus, a parent could say to his child, "You need to participate in a sport; which one would you like to try this school year?" In this situation the parent provides the general requirement that the child be physically active, but gives the child the freedom to choose the activity that will accomplish the goal. Setting reasonable expectations, being emotionally sensitive to and engaged in a child's feelings, creating a stable environment for childhood, and supporting the child's goals… these are ingredients for the winning formula.

- ✓ Life for children in the late 20th and early 21st centuries has opened up many opportunities that were previously not available to children.
- ✓ Striking the right balance among academics, extracurricular activities, and unstructured child-driven play should be a major goal for parents.
- ✓ Children benefit from a balanced approach to their activities throughout childhood.
- ✓ Goals to optimize a child's time and energies are outlined.

CHAPTER SEVEN
Parenting Obstacles that Make
Can/Should Decisions Difficult

Sometimes things just get in the way of good decisions.

Parents today face a number of can/should decisions that our parents and grandparents did not face. Hopefully, the information in this book will give parents the information, help and confidence to make many of these tough decisions for their children. My goal is to focus and ease the decision process. I believe that an informed, confident parent is likely to be a great parent.

A parent trap is an assumption or belief
that interferes with a parent's ability to
incorporate a core function or value
into parenting.

Unfortunately, I often encounter parents who have difficulty implementing good parenting decisions because of various obstacles that I call parent traps. A parent trap is an assumption or belief that interferes with a parent's ability to incorporate a core function or value into parenting. In my 32 years of pediatric practice, I have witnessed many families succumb to these parent traps. These parents are intelligent and well-meaning adults who let these traps become impediments to being the most effective parents they can be.

Below is my list of parent traps that readers should avoid as they make the important parenting decisions we have discussed in this book. Every parent flirts with some these traps at one time or another. When one of these traps begins to color decision-making, trouble begins. I hope that an awareness of these traps will enable parents to avoid them.

Doc Smo's List of Parent Traps

Parent Trap One: Age-inappropriate and other inappropriate expectations.

Parents almost universally see their children as exceptional and want to provide all the opportunities possible for their children's success. Consequently, some parents introduce their children to experiences that the children are developmentally too young to participate in. For example, when children are asked to master academics or are enrolled in sports before they are developmentally ready and with the expectation that they will become superstar students or athletes, the results can be negative for both children and parents.

When the child fails to perform or simply loses interest and energy for the activity, both the parent and the child are disappointed. The parent trap here is inappropriate parental expectations. With more realistic parental expectations, this story would probably have had a happier ending. The child may have gained a love of learning or acquired some valuable athletic skills from the experiences that they enjoyed without burnout and disappointed expectations. Sports participation for children has benefits beyond winning: children who play sports learn teamwork; they also learn to work toward goals bigger than themselves, sacrifice for others, win or lose gracefully, and deal with disappointment. All of these experiences will make them more resilient, balanced adults. Additionally, parents enjoy the process far more without placing the pressure of constant achievement on themselves and their children.

Parent Trap Two: More is not always better.

How do we define success for our children? Parents should ask themselves this core question as they struggle with every parenting decision they make. My wife and I felt that we achieved success when we set realistically high standards for our children, provided them with plenty of opportunities to experience a wide variety of activities, allowed them to cultivate their own interests and talents, provided them with their "needs" and some of their "wants," and hit the right balance between work and play. I think many of today's parents have trouble with balancing the needs/wants decisions as well as the work/play balance aspect of their children's lives. When we assume that more is always better, we often fall into Parent Trap Two.

For example, when parents perceive the world in competitive terms, they often overs-schedule their children with activities. They hope that participation in a wide range of activities will give their children an edge. Unfortunately, too many structured activities deprive children of much needed time to play, learn to relate to their peers, and explore their own creativity. While children who participate in lots of activities get experiences that other children may not, they also lose unstructured playtime that is important for their development. Children love such time because it offers them the opportunity to explore the world on their own terms; wherever the children's interests want to go that day is where the play will take them. Not so for structured activities, especially if adults are orchestrating the show.

Again, many children whose parents are fortunate enough to have a good income over-indulge their children with material things. Trying to meet all of a child's wants is not natural or sustainable. What happens to these children when they grow up and struggle to meet their own basic needs? They may experience a sense of overwhelming failure, that's what may happen. As a result of this parenting trap, many children are ill-equipped to deal with denial as adults; consequently, they often make poor economic decisions when resources become scarce. They have never learned to prioritize their wants. Such children have a difficult time judging the worth of things.

Parents must master limit-setting sooner rather than later!

Parent Trap Three: Limit-setting is unpleasant.

Many parents find setting limits for their children quite unpleasant—as unpleasant as their children do.

Unfortunately, setting limits is one of the most important parenting tasks. In fact, next to loving, feeding, and protecting children, limit setting is probably the most important function of parenting. Enforcing boundaries is uncomfortable because it often results in conflict between parent and child. On the other hand, failing to define and enforce boundaries with children is a mistake. Any parent who is unwilling to endure conflict will have difficulty setting limits. Children who are raised without appropriate limits are frequently bound for trouble as they grow older; firm, consistent boundaries that allow for reasonable exploration are best. If parents have not established good boundaries for their children, how can they insist that their children be responsible with money, eat good quality food, accept some responsibility with respect to their family, or resist the over-indulgence that every child craves? The answer is that they can't. Setting reasonable and concrete boundaries for children is the pillar of effective parenting.

Parents must master limit-setting sooner rather than later! How does a parent go about setting effective limits? Chapter Five describes "demanding and warm" as the best parenting style. Demanding is the limit setting part of equation. Demanding means setting reasonable limits with clear consequences for failure. We all know this instinctively. So where do parents trip up in limit-setting? The following are some of the most common ways.

Unsuccessful limit-setting styles:

The Beggar: These parents beg their children to behave or comply with their wishes. Begging is a common style of communication with children: "Oh honey, please do this or that. Oh honey, please don't do that." Parents can speak politely to their children without begging them to obey.

The Hollow Threat: These parents threaten limits but do not enforce them: "Honey, if you do that one more time I am really going to get angry." This style teaches children that the parent is not going to do what he or she threatens. This is worse than poor limit-setting—this parent has abdicated his or her authority by failing to follow through with consequences. Children's love and respect for parents and their authority are powerful tools in the limit-setting arena. Parents should never give them up!

Parenting by Proxy: Some parents whom I knew hosted a party for their teenage child and provided alcohol for the teenage guests, even though they had not yet reached legal drinking age. When I asked the father if he thought providing alcohol for teens was appropriate, he responded that he'd rather his child's friends drink in his home where he could supervise them rather than out on their own. He added that other families were doing the same thing and they saw nothing wrong with it. Well, that settles that. This father forfeited his decisions to his child's friends and their parents. That's what I call parenting by proxy.

Parent Trap 4: "What is mine is mine and what is yours is mine."

This trap is a variation on a parent's failure to set limits. Children sometimes fail to recognize that their parents' property, time, money, and privacy are not theirs. Such children have no sense of gratitude. When the lines of distinction between what is theirs and what is their parents' are blurred, conflict is inevitable.

For example, I often see parents waiting in my office entertain their children with games or movies on the parent's iPhone or iPpad. Once when I entered an exam room, a child threw his mother's iPhone across the room. He threw a $600 device that was not his across the room because he was annoyed at having his video game interrupted! I was shocked that this behavior did not seem to perturb the child's mother. The parent's reaction—or lack thereof—disturbed me more than the child's behavior.

When my children were teenagers, I saw many of their schoolmates driving cars that any adult would envy. Often, these cars were nicer than the cars their parents drove. Even if a family can afford to provide such expensive vehicles, I see no value in doing so. Ironically, intelligent, responsible adults frequently seem unable to set appropriate limits and boundaries for their children. Many of these parents probably drove nice cars and felt guilty requiring their children to drive less luxurious vehicles. What is mine (the parent's) is yours (the child's), right? I wonder how these parents react when those expensive cars get their inevitable bangs and scrapes from their inexperienced teenage drivers.

Parent Trap 5: "If my child fails, I as a parent have failed."

Failure is key to learning. Many parents want their children to become successful adults without ever experiencing failure. Shielding children from the consequences of lack of effort, bad decisions, sloppy work, lack of practice, and so forth is shortsighted. The sting of failure or the negative feedback from adults is often the best teacher. Many parents feel that if their children fail, they as parents have failed. I have a totally different view. Helping children learn from their failures is a parent's role. Parents should teach their children to learn from their failures when they are young and the consequences are relatively benign. The older children are when they learn to take responsibility for their mistakes, the worse the consequences may be.

Helping children learn from their failures is a parent's role.

For example, Johnny waits until the last minute to complete his schoolwork. He is a fifth grader who generally does well in school. Unfortunately, the assignment that he has known about for the past three weeks is due tomorrow, and he hasn't started to work on it. Desperate and distraught, he goes to his parents for help. Should his parents rescue him and do his project for him the night before it is due or should they make him put together whatever he can and suffer the consequences for his procrastination? His parents have a great opportunity to allow Johnny to experience the consequences of procrastination while he is young enough not to suffer too much from his failure. The point is that Johnny's failure is not his parents' failure. If Johnny gets to high school or college without learning the consequences of procrastination, the consequences are likely to be much more severe and long lasting. Let children learn about failure when they are young and the consequences are not life altering.

Parent Trap 6: You are my everything!

Parenting is one of the most important jobs of our lives, but it is not the only job. It is possible to become so consumed by our parenting role that other aspects of our lives begin to suffer: our marriages, careers, and even our own individuality and personal growth.

For example, I have noticed that parental divorce frequently follows the birth of a second child. While many reasons contribute to this phenomenon, I think the feeling of isolation and loss of romance that having two children entail contributes to it. Fathers initiate divorce in this situation more than mothers. Fathers more often feel the loss of romance and excitement. Many fathers resent the fact that life after children is so radically different than before they were born. Children are important, their needs are important, but they are not the only needs a family has. Parents should resist the temptation to make their children the center of everything, thereby jeopardizing other aspects of family life.

When any aspect of our life becomes all-consuming, we may become less interesting, well-rounded individuals. This is true of parenting as well. Some parents lose perspective when it comes to their children. When their child leaves the nest, such parents experience a heavier fall than their friends.

Parent Trap 7: Preferring "friendship" to respect.

This trap is another variation of failure to set limits. We all love our children and want to treat them with respect, but treating them as equals with the belief that they will like us is a mistake. Of course, we should always treat everyone, especially our children, with respect, but that doesn't mean we can't make the rules and enforce them. Parents should strive to be loving, fair, engaged, and committed to their children's well-being. Parents should be leaders of rather than friends to their children.

The example that comes to mind is the mother who dresses like her teenage daughter. Such parents are trying to appear chic and hip before their daughters. Mothers are supposed to be role models for their daughters, not vice versa. Parents are not their children's peers; they have a great deal more life experience and wisdom than children.

Parents should be leaders of rather than friends to their children.

Another example of inappropriate identification with children is the father who loses all perspective when it comes to the subject of sports and his children, especially his sons. He forgets that one of the great things about sports participation is that, despite everyone's best efforts, someone is going to win and someone is going to lose. Learning to do both of these graciously is one of the valuable life lessons that sports provide. When a father fails to be gracious about the winning/losing process or becomes overly involved in the outcome of a sporting event, he will eventually lose the respect of his child. Children want parents to provide support and encouragement for their participation without irrational prejudice toward an opposing player or team.

Parent Trap 8: Do as I say, not as I do!

I think we all instinctively relate to this trap. Children listen to what parents tell them but their behavior is more likely to be altered by what parents do rather than what they say. Children are born knowing how to imitate. Think about a toddler who goes around repeating words he hears, pretending to do the things he sees others doing, and reproducing what he has seen in their play. Imitation is a child's main way of learning, so you want to make sure that the things your children see are things you want them to imitate.

For example, parents who fail to conform their own behavior to a strong moral compass frequently have children who struggle with right and wrong. . Ethical behavior does not come naturally; children learn it from their parents and other adults in their lives. As an example of this, I am reminded of the occasional family I see where the father openly demonstrates little respect for his wife's feelings or opinion. I am often part of some heated exchanges between husband and wife, usually with Junior in the room. I personally have not witnessed any physical violence in this situation, but certainly these Dads are exhibiting a large degree of disrespect for their wives. The behavior that Dad is modeling for his children is, in my opinion, destructive. I have personally seen some of these children grow to threaten and demean their mothers as they become teens.

Imitation is a child's main way of learning so you want to make sure that the things your children see are things you want them to imitate.

Unfortunately, teenage boys physically threatening their mothers is a common event during the mid teen years;

sadly, their fathers modeled this behavior for them. "Do as I say" just can't overcome the messages these boys get from observing the demeaning way their mothers have been treated by their fathers.

Parenting Obstacles that Get in the Way of Good Can/Should Decisions

✓ Parents making age inappropriate expectations.

✓ Parents who provide too many wants.

✓ Parents who avoid limit setting because the process is unpleasant for everyone.

✓ Parents who blur the line between their children's needs and wants.

✓ Parents shielding their children from failure

✓ Parents sacrificing their own development for their children.

✓ Parents who want their children's approval at any cost.

✓ Parents who say one thing but do another.

Paul Smolen, MD

CHAPTER EIGHT
Summary

Life in the digital age is different.

We live in the information age, a time when facts, figures, and opinions are literally a millisecond away. With a touch of the mouse, we can answer questions that took lengthy research in huge libraries to answer just a generation ago. Gathering a lot of information, asking the right questions, and acting on the answers are the biggest hurdles that today's parents must overcome. In today's world our children can do things that were unimaginable things just a few decades ago with amazing ease, but should we allow them to? Just because they can doesn't mean they should. Differentiating the Cans from the Shoulds is the essence of this book. I hope that it helps parents to find their own answers for their unique children.

Finding the right balance of can and should is different for every family and perhaps every child. Few absolutes exist when it comes to human behavior and family dynamics. For instance, for most families the advice from experts is to limit screen time to one or two hours per day, but what if a child has physical handicaps that make screens an integral part of his day? What if a child has exceptional curiosity such that pursuit of her passions and talents necessitates a more intense life with computers and screens? Parents are best positioned to assess the true needs of their children. My intention in writing this book is to pose the questions, point out where decisions need to be made, and give the parents relevant information which will help them think through each decision. Families are as unique as the individuals that compose them. Clearly this is a situation where one-size-fits-all does not apply.

Knowledge is power when it comes to parenting.

Informed parents will make informed decisions for their children. As the great leader of the British Empire in the 19th century Benjamin Disraeli (1804-1881) pointed out, "We are not creatures of circumstance." Said another way, those who are able to make decisions for themselves often relieve themselves of having circumstances imposed on them. To a large degree, informed people create their own destiny. This is especially true when it comes to parenting. An informed, thoughtful parent is likely to be a great parent who blesses her children with wisdom and raises them under the umbrella of secure limits, loving guidance, and reasonable expectations.

Parents are making choices all the time, and these choices have consequences--both immediate and long-term. Often we will spend a lot of effort researching which washing machine to buy for our home or which car is the best value; shouldn't we spend as much effort to decide what to feed our children or whether to put a TV in their room? In the long run, parenting decisions will have far more important consequences for children's lives than the purchase of an appliance or car. These decisions deserve as much or more thought as the smaller choices that we make all the time!

All the families I have cared for during my pediatric career undoubtedly love their children, but some have major difficulty acting on what, intellectually, they may understand is best for their children. To illustrate this point, I am reminded of a family whose parents worked long hours involving frequent travel. At the children's checkup, the subject of their nutrition came up. Their sons' diet consisted almost entirely of processed food including lots of sweet cereals, sugary drinks, and processed meats. Their children were eating poorly, and I knew the parents could afford to provide a better diet. I made some relatively simple suggestions to improve the family's diet that met with the mother's understanding and approval. Did this knowledge and encouragement change her behavior...NO! I really think this mother understood that she was making important choices for her family that might have a negative impact on their long term health, but she was falling for parent trap #7: "Honey, I want you to like me" thinking. She continued doing what she felt her children wanted even though she understood that this was not in their long-term best interest.

Sometimes, however, the opposite happens. Last summer I did a check-up of a thirteen-year-old young man in the ordinary fashion. Anybody who provides healthcare for thirteen-year-old boys knows that a major health topic for them is safety and accidents. Young teens tend to exhibit a dangerous combination of desire for thrills, great physical agility, high energy, a sense of invulnerability, and bad judgment. During visits with young teens, I always make sure to talk about wearing a helmet while biking or rolling around on anything. With this particular patient, we had the usual conversation and that was that. Later in the summer, his father, who had brought him to the appointment and had heard our conversation, called to thank me for reinforcing his use of a bike helmet. After his visit, this boy had had a bad crash on his bicycle in which his helmet was destroyed, but he was essentially uninjured. He chose to wear his helmet when riding that day, and thank goodness he did. Choices parents—and their children—make do have consequences often steering good fortune toward or away from them and their family. The choices that parents make...well, those are their choices.

Now that you understand more of the Shoulds, you are better equipped to make informed decisions about the Cans in your child's day-to-day life.

Sometimes, well-intentioned parents do not create the ideal environment for their children to become independent, happy, productive, self-sufficient adults. Surprisingly, many of these parents are unaware that some of their parenting choices are not ideal. Some of these families have simply not taken the time to think about the choices they are making. Many families are taking the course of least resistance in their decision making, while others are letting the excitement and thrills of the Cans take precedence over the more balanced Shoulds.

Much of what parents need to do is unpleasant. Setting limits, saying no, and being more persistent than a tenacious ten- year-old is both difficult and time consuming. Some parents simply can't set limits well, but more often they just don't understand how important that limit-setting is. I hate to see genuinely well-intentioned parents make decisions that I know they would never make if they had more information and knowledge. My hope is that when your children come at you with the inevitable, "Why not?" your retort won't need to be, "Because I said so," and instead will be a list of good, sound reasons you used to set that particular boundary. To me, that is true parent power. If you were a child, which answer would garner more respect for your parents: "Because I said so" or "Because I know better, I want what's best for you, and here's why you can't"?

Demanding but warm... the best parenting style.

As we saw in Chapter Four, the combination of the demanding but warm parenting style seems the best guarantor of raising balanced, successful children.

- Demanding, in the parenting context, means setting high expectations and holding children responsible for their actions.

    ✓ Demanding parents are likely to produce children who take responsibility for their actions and set high goals. Regarding the "spheres" that this book addresses, successful parenting results in eating food of high nutritional value, achieving high academic standards, accepting responsibilities of family membership, and learning to make good financial decisions.

- Demanding does not mean setting unrealistically high goals for children.

    ✓ As this book demonstrates, the end game in these families is often not pretty. Moreover, demanding does not mean making age inappropriate expectations for a child. Pushing a child too hard in order to achieve a particular goal or skill, especially if they are not developmentally ready for it, will simply frustrate them and slow down their natural emotional development.

- First and foremost, warm translates to unconditional love and acceptance.

    ✓ That doesn't mean accepting bad behavior, but rather letting children know that they are loved despite failures and shortcomings. This assurance is the powerful wind behind the sails that buoys children up during troubled times. It creates resiliency and is fundamental to raising emotionally healthy children.

- Warm also means being emotionally engaged with children: listening and empathizing with their feelings.

    ✓ Parents must be engaged with their children in order for their children to grow emotionally. Not only does this emotional intimacy bond children to their parents, but it also gives parents an opportunity to provide moral guidance and perspective, something children desperately need. Listening and trying to understand whatever feelings a child is experiencing demonstrates respect for the child and empowers the child.

- Warm doesn't mean indulging children with all or even most of their wants.

  ✓ We all want to please our children, but providing them with too much "stuff," including electronics, processed food, leisure time, lack of family responsibility, or money is not what warm means. While unpleasant, setting limits is better for children than indulging their immediate wants and desires.

- Warm does not mean shielding children from failure.

  ✓ Failure is an essential ingredient in learning. It is unnatural never to fail. Children rarely get straight A's all through school or never lose at sports or other competitions. Parents who refuse to let their children fail often inhibit ultimate success for their children.

- Warm does not mean that parents should treat children as equals or friends.

  ✓ Enjoying experiences together is great, but when parents start to perceive their children as equal captains of the USS Family, serious trouble is on the horizon. Parents need to be the adults in the house because they are the only ones in the family with an adult perspective and experiences broad enough to make difficult decisions. Warm definitely doesn't mean giving children's wishes equal importance to that of parents'.

What I hope you will take away from this book.

In parenting as in other aspects of life, we must understand the questions before we can find answers. In this book, I have posed the questions that I think are important, and I have provided information to answer them.

Whether the sphere is nutrition, diet, family responsibility, money, or life balance, knowledge is power. By reading this book, you have invested the time to learn about some of the latest pediatric research. Now it is time use that information to benefit your family.

You should start with the sphere that is most important to your family and then slowly move through the other spheres of decisions that we have discussed.

If your children are old enough, family meetings can be a great way to set goals and implement strategies to achieve those that are most important to your family.

Trust your instincts when using what you have learned. The line between Can and Should is different for every family. I am confident that you will make the best decisions for your family because no one has more invested in your children's ultimate success and well-being than you!

Paul Smolen, MD

About the Author

Dr. Paul Smolen, also known as *Doc Smo* by his friends, is a graduate of Duke University (1974), Rutgers Medical School (1978), and Wake Forest University-N.C. Baptist Hospital (1982). At Wake Forest University he completed a residency in general pediatrics, served as chief resident, and completed a fellowship in ambulatory pediatrics. Subsequently, he became board certified in the American Academy of Pediatrics (1983) and completed his maintenance of certification in 2014.

For the last 33 years, he has been an Adjunct Associate Professor of Pediatrics at the University of North Carolina-Chapel Hill, helping to train a generation of medical students and pediatric residents as well as author numerous research papers. He is currently a practicing pediatrician in Charlotte, NC.

Doc Smo is a bona-fide expert in knowing what parents want and need to know about parenting and child health. He shares practical and useful advice with parents and children alike, firmly believing that "an informed parent is a great parent."

Whether teaching, practicing, blogging or writing, Doc Smo's mission is to improve the health and well-being of children.

Paul Smolen, MD

WORKS CITED

"Allowance Tips: Good Money Management Begins with an Allowance." National PTA Family Education Staff. <http://life.familyeducation.com/allowance/parenting/36441.html#ixzz2gcJ0hT5t>.

American Academy of Pediatrics "Policy Statement: Breastfeeding and the Use of Human Milk." Pediatrics 115 (2012): 496.

Bertini, Giovanna, Carlo Dani, Michele Tronchin, Firmino F. Rubaltelli. "Is Breastfeeding Really Favoring Early Neonatal Jaundice?" Pediatrics 107 (March 2001): 41. <http://www.pediatricsdigest.mobi/content/107/3/e41.short>.

Black, R. "Micronutrient Deficiency — an Underlying Cause of Morbidity and Mortality." Bulletin of the World Health Organization 81 January 2003.

Bronson, Po and Ashley Merryman. Nuture Shock. New York: Twelve, 2009, Chapter 2.

Brown A. "Media use by children younger than 2 years." Pediatrics 128:5 (November) 1040-5.

Caplow, Theodore, Louis Hicks, and Ben J. Wattenberg. The First Measured Century. Washington: AEI Press, 2001.

"Children eating more, and more frequently outside the home." ScienceDaily, 25 Jul. 2011. Web. 22 Sep. 2013.

College Board. <https://trends.collegeboard.org/home>.

Elkind, David. The Hurried Child. 3rd ed. New York: Da Capo, 2007.

Fox, Mary Kay, M.Ed; Susan Pac, M.S., R.D.; Barbara Devaney, PhD; Linda Jankowski,

M.S. "Feeding Infants and Toddlers Study: What Foods Are Infants and Toddlers Eating?" Journal of the American Dietician Association (2004).

"Fast Food and Childhood Allergies." <u>UK Guardian on the Web</u> Jan. 2014 <http://www.guardian.co.uk/lifeandstyle/2013/jan/14/fast-food-child- asthma-allergies.html>.

Ford, C., D. Ward, and M. White. "Television viewing associated with adverse dietary outcomes in children ages 2-6." <u>Obesity Review</u>. 13:12 (December 2012) 1139-47.

Fredricks, Jennifer A. and Jacquelynne S. Eccles. "Is extracurricular participation associated with beneficial outcomes? Concurrent and longitudinal relations." <u>Developmental Psychology</u> 42:4 (Jul 2006): 698-713.

Fung et al. "Incidence of and Mortality From Coronary Heart Disease and Stroke in Women." <u>Circulation</u> 119 (2009): 1093-1100.

Ginsburg K. "The Importance of Play in Promoting Healthy Child Development and maintaining Strong Parent-Child Bonds." <u>Pediatrics</u> 119: 1 (January 2007): 183.

Guran T., and A. Bereket. "International epidemic of childhood obesity and television viewing." <u>Minerva Pediatrics</u>. 63:6 (December 2011) 483-90.

Holick, Michael F., M.D., Ph.D. "Vitamin D Deficiency." <u>New England Journal of Medicine</u> 357 (July 2007): 266-281 <http://www.nejm.org/doi/full/10.1056/NEJMra070553>.

Howell, Ryan T., Ph.D. <u>Can't Buy Happiness? Money, personality, and well-being</u>. <http://www.psychologytoday.com/blog/cant-buy-happiness>.

Huston, A.C. et al. <u>Big World, Small Screen: The Role of Television in American Society</u>. Lincoln: University of Nebraska Press, 1992.

<u>Info Please</u>. "State Compulsory School Attendance Laws." <http://www.infoplease.com/ipa/A0112617.html>.

"Is Cooking Really Cheaper than Fast Food?" <http://www.motherjones.com/tom-philpott/2011/10/cooking-really- cheaper-junk-food-mark-bittman>.

Johnson, et al. "Dietary Sugars Intake and Cardiovascular Health." <u>Circulation</u> 20:11 (September 15, 2009): 1011-1020.

Jyoti, Christine R. and Learn Vest. "Why it costs so much to raise a kid: The typical middle-income family will spend $235,000 raising a child to age 17. Here are some of the ways that cost adds up." <http://money.msn.com/family-money/why-it-costs-so-much-to-raise-a- kid>.

"Kids and money." CNN Money Online, Lesson 12, 2014. <http://money.cnn.com/magazines/moneymag/money101/lesson12/i ndex5.htm>.

Manganello, Jennifer A. and Catherine A. Taylor. "Television Exposure as a Risk Factor for Aggressive Behavior Among 3-Year-Old Children." Pediatrics and Adolescent Medicine, 163 (11): 1037 (2009).

Marketingvox. "Rand Youth Poll." Seventeen, September 8, 2012. <http://www.statisticbrain.com/teenage-consumer-spending-statistics/>.

McCann, D. "Food Additives and Hyperactive Behaviour in 3 year olds and 8/9 year old children in the Community; randomized, double-blinded, placebo trial." Lancet 117 (2008) 1216-1217.

McCarthy, E. "Pediatricians and Television: It's Time to Rethink Our Messaging and Our Efforts." Pediatrics 131: 3 (March 1, 2013) 589-590.

McGill H., C. MccMahan, S. Gidding. "Preventing Heart Disease in the 21st Century: Implications of the Pathobiological Determinants of Atherosclerosis in Youth (PDAY) Study." Circulation 117 (2008): 1216-1227.

Media Use by Children Younger Than 2 Years, American Academy of Pediatrics Policy Statement. Pediatrics (October 17, 2011). <http://pediatrics.aappublications.org/content/early/2011/10/12/peds.2011-1753>.

Medina, John. Brain Rules for Babies. New York: Pear Press (2010), 361-367.

"NCAA Statistics." Business Insider. Feb. 2012. <http://www.businessinsider.com/odds-college-athletes-become-professionals-2012-2?op=1>.

Poti, Jennifer M. and Barry M. Popkin. "Trends in energy intake among US children by eating location and food source, 1977-2006." Journal of the American Dietetic Association, 111: 8 (August 2011).

Powell C., B. Ngyuyen, E. Han. "Energy Intake from Restaurants." American Journal of Preventative Medicine 43: 5 (November 2012) 498-504.

Rideout, V. J., U. G. Foehr, and D. F. Roberts. Generation M2: Media in the Lives of 8- to 18-Year-Olds. Menlo Park, CA: Kaiser Family Foundation (2010).

"Report of the Task Force on the Family." Pediatrics 111: 2 (June 1, 2003). <http://pediatrics.aappublications.org/content/111/

Supplement_2/1541.full?sid=4197c8ae-2eb4-4730-8f6e-ae458d95d7d>.

Shah, Anup. "Children as Consumers." Global Issues. 21 Nov. 2010. Web. 30 Sep. 2013. <http://www.globalissues.org/article/237/children-as-consumers>.

Singh, et al. "Effect of Indo-Mediterranean Diet on Progression of Coronary Artery Disease in High Risk Patients." 360 (November 2002): 1455-1461.

Smolen, Paul, M.D. "Bedtime Bliss for Everyone." DocSmo.com <http://www.docsmo.com/bedtime-bliss-for-everyone>. December, 2013, Episode 123.

Smolen, Paul, M.D. "Children; Eating Themselves Sick." DocSmo.com <http://www.docsmo.com/children-eating-themselves-sick>.

Smolen, Paul, M.D. "Fast Food: More Bad News." DocSmo.com <http://www.docsmo.com/fast-food-more-bad-news-article-edited>.

Smolen, Paul, M.D. "College Savings Made Easy." DocSmo.com, <http://www.docsmo.com/college-savings-made-easy-pedcast/>.

Smolen, Paul, M.D. "Why Your Child Should Avoid Sugary Drinks." DocSmo.com <http://www.docsmo.com/why-your-child-should-avoid-sugary-drinks>.

Strasburger, Victor C., Amy B. Jordan, Ed Donnerstein. "Health Effects of Media on Children and Adolescents." Pediatrics 125: 4 (April 1, 2010) 756-767.

The National Center for Education Statistics. "Rate of Illiteracy circa 1900." <http://nces.ed.gov/naal/lit_history.asp>.

Trelease, Jim. The Read Aloud Handbook. New York: Penguin Books, 5th edition 2006.

Trichopoulou, Antonia, M.D., Tina Costacou, Ph.D., Christina Bamia, Ph.D., and Dimitrios Trichopoulos, M.D. "Adherence to a Mediterranean Diet and Survival in a Greek Population." New England Journal Medicine 348 (June 26, 2003): 348:2599-2608. <http://www.nejm.org/doi/full/10.1056/NEJMoa025039>.

UltimateCalculators.com <http://www.ultimatecalculators.com/compound_interest_calculator.html, <http://www.psychologytoday.com/blog/cant-buy- happiness/201301/what-is-happiness-five-characteristics-happy-people>.

United States. Centers for Disease Control. Consumption of Added Sugar Among U.S. Children and Adolescents. Washington: GPO, 2012.

United States. Centers for Disease Control. Vitamin D Supplementation and Breasting. Washington: GPO, 2009. <http://www.cdc.gov/breastfeeding/recommendations/vitamin_d.html>.

United States. Census Bureau. Washington: GPO, 2010.

United States. USDA: Dietary Guidelines for Americans 2010. Washington: GPO, 2010.

United States. U.S. Department of Labor: 100 Years of U.S. Consumer Spending

Washington: GPO, May 2006. <http://www.bls.gov/opub/uscs/report991.pdf>.

Vaillant, George. Triumphs of Experience. Boston: Harvard, 2012.

"Vitamin D." Mayo Clinic Online Health Guide. Nov. 2013. <http://www.mayoclinic.org/drugs-supplements/vitamin- d/evidence/>.

Wright, J.C., A.C. Huston, K.C. Murphy, et al. "The relations of early television viewing to school readiness and vocabulary of children from low-income families: the early window project. Child Development. 2001:7 ( ).

Wright, J.C., A. C. Huston, K. C. Murphy, M. St Peters, M. Pinon, R. Scantlin, J. Kotler. "The relations of early television viewing to school readiness and vocabulary of children from low-income families: the early window project." Child Development 72:5 (September-October 2001) 1347-66.

Ybarra et. al. "Linkages between internet and other media violence with seriously violent behavior by youth." Pediatrics. 122:5 (November 2008) 929-37.

Zimmerman, F. J., D. A. Christakis, and A. N. Meltzoff. "Associations between Media Viewing and Language Development in Children Under Age 2 Years." The Journal of Pediatrics 151:4 (date) 364-368.

CPSIA information can be obtained
at www.ICGtesting.com
Printed in the USA
FFOW04n0922080316
22059FF